NO REASON TO LIVE

1971-1999

1999-

SCOTT MASON

No Reason To Live

Printed in the United States of America
ISBN: 10: 1460968980
ISBN: 13: 978-1460968987

Learn more information at:
www.scottmason.org

WARNING

When I started to write this book, I felt I needed someone to help me. I sat down and wrote out all the reasons why I couldn't do this on my own. I was kicked out of three high schools in a very short period of time and I obtained a G.E.D in one of the worst prisons in the country. English was one of my worst subjects throughout school and my grammar shows it. But I figured if God can use a donkey to speak to Balaam, He sure can guide me in writing this book. And He did just that.

The process of writing for the most part went very smoothly. The days that it did not were because I tried to do it in my own hand and not God's. I learned very quickly that He must guide me and not the other way around! Once I was finished I sent it off to my editor with one stipulation. I needed him to edit this book consistent with the way that I talk in everyday life. My editor has known me for 10 years and he is a great friend, so I didn't think this would be much of a problem. It turned out to be a big problem. Editors are taught to edit by the industry standard; so when I came along with my manuscript and stipulation, he had to throw a lot of what he knows out the window. We went back and forth quite a bit to get this book the way I wanted it to come across. When it was finally completed it he told me that, "he is never going to edit another book as long as he lives!" Of course he was kidding, or at least I hope he was.

Why was it so important to me to have this book sound like me and not some graduate student? It's because that's not who I am. I am so thankful for all the people I get to help day in and day out. But I get the chance to help them because I am real about who I am. There are no games with me. I tell it like I see it and I am not worried about what someone might think of me. Maybe that gets me into a little trouble at times but the reward of being able to serve God is so worth it.

So what is the "warning" I am offering? It's simply this. If you see words in this book that are spelled differently than you are accustomed to, or maybe you see sentences that start with the word "And" or "But" it is because I asked the editor to keep it that way. And if you read words that seem crass, I am only trying to authentically help you catch exactly the way it was. I think it was hard for the editor to leave some of these things alone or leave some of these things in, but I am so thankful that he did.

I hope you enjoy reading about my life and seeing my heart for God's people. I do ask one thing of you as the reader though. If this book touches you in any way, please pass it along to someone you might think would also benefit from it.

Scott Mason

CONTENTS

Foreward

I met Scott Mason shortly after his final release from prison. He was looking for a church home and wandered into the church where I served as senior pastor on a Wednesday night. Our primary ministries on Wednesday nights were to children and youth; but we also had an adult, "prayer and praise" group of 20-30 that met in one of the, "upper rooms." I'm not sure how Scott even found us that night. It wasn't exactly the best setting to just jump into church life, but Scott did his best to endure it. He left as quickly as he came; and I never really thought I would see him again.

Little did I know that we would become dear friends in a relationship that is still very much alive today. For several years, Scott and Carrie lived less than two blocks from Marlene and me. I am sure many must have thought of Scott and me as the, "odd couple". But we were (and are) brothers in Christ who were both deeply concerned with how to share the love of Jesus with a hurting world. I sort of was the, "inside man" on the job, and he the, "outside man."

To this day, Scott and I talk at least several times a week. I had the privilege of marrying him and Carrie and dedicating their daughters. It was from Scott that I stole the phrase, "God is good; everyone else is suspect." If he ever copyrights it, I will owe him a bundle! But in reality, I already owe him a lot. Scott has a deep heart to help others, and I have been the recipient of that help too. Whether it's a new pair of shoes because he thinks mine are getting a little beat up or an autographed, "Lem Barney" jersey because he thinks my office is pretty boring, Scott loves to give. I have seen him give his last $20 so a homeless man could have lunch and some supplies.

But what Scott loves and longs to give the most is the gift of grace and hope that comes through Jesus Christ. He is a Christ-follower who gets easily frustrated with the lip service only faith often found in the institutional church. But despite his frustration, he continues to serve, with a delightful focus on the hurting, the broken, the outsiders. He is determined to make faith real. I love him for that!

Scott will often say, "Miller, I've been coming to you for advice for almost 10 years; and you haven't given me any yet!" Aside from the fact that I don't have all that much to give, I don't often give it because Scott has a heart to hear from God. Like all of us straining to hear the voice of the Spirit, consistent with the truth of God's Word, Scott sometimes misses it. And more than once, as he shares in this book, he has run ahead of the Lord's timing when he does hear God's voice. But Scott never gives up. And probably more than anyone I know- when Scott truly hears God's voice, he obeys regardless of the cost.

To watch Scott grow in the faith has been an incredible privilege for my wife Marlene and me. (And to see Carrie put up with him all these years has been pretty cool too!) To see the rough edges of his life begin to be smoothed by the sandpaper in God's loving hand has been a privilege too. His example of faithfulness has been a genuine encouragement.

I commend this book to all because I believe it too will be an encouragement. Scott simply tells his story in this book, and there is much to glean from it. It is both incredibly unique, and yet filled with the stuff we all face in some form or another at the same time. Maybe you are reading this as a hurting parent or grandparent whose son or daughter or grandchild is living life on the edge. Maybe you are reading this as a frustrated Christ-follower who wonders if it's, "worth it." Maybe you are reading this as a rebel on the run who deep down is a little scared and a lot empty. Maybe you are reading this as someone simply looking for some sense of direction or hope in your hurting world.

To all such readers and many more I say, "Keep reading to the end." And see if God by His Spirit doesn't use stories from Scott's life to challenge you with fresh direction for yours! God is good...

Tim Miller

Senior Pastor- Cornerstone Alliance Church, Marion OH

February 2011

ONE
DETROIT AND BEYOND

How did you grow up? What was your family like? Did your mom and dad care? These questions are the ones adults ask me the most; and I think it's because they know that if all this could happen to my mom and dad it could happen to them. I didn't grow up in the hood. I didn't grow up with parents who beat me. I didn't grow up in the stereotypical environment the experts say often leads to a life of crime. For me, it was just the opposite.

I am not too sure how old I was when my parents divorced, but I couldn't have more than 5 years of age. I never really cared to know the exact date anyway. It's not like Hallmark has a card for that type of situation. Maybe they should though. All I know is that one minute I am living with my mom and dad and the next I am only seeing my dad every other weekend. I am pretty sure that this was all confusing to me, but being so young I guess I just went with the flow of things. It wasn't like they sat me down and told me what was going on. So I just figured it out on my own.

My mom had a very hard life growing up. Her father was an alcoholic and was never home; and when he was he was pretty abusive. Her mom had to work two and three jobs just to keep the heat on and food on the table. And my mom as a teen had to take care of the house and watch her sisters. This is important to note because it shows why my mom worked so hard and why she was always on me to stay in school and become the best I could be. She never wanted me to live like she grew up, so she made sure that I wouldn't have to live that way either by pursuing a college degree. I am not really sure why my parents divorced, but I think a lot had to do with my mom wanting something more for her life than being a housewife like a lot of women were back in the 1970's. My dad wanted her to be a stay at home mom. But that is neither here nor there. Being a single mom is hard on any woman, but being a single mom and having to work full time and attend college is even harder. My mom always had to work, so a lot of people had their hand in watching me. I was either at one of three grandma's houses or I was with my aunts. So between my dad's house every other weekend and my grandma's houses or aunt's houses the rest of the time, I became what I call a kid with a bunch of moms and dads- more moms than dads. And it really sucked. Each person had different rules at their house, and for a little kid it is hard enough to deal with one set of rules let alone five. But I dealt with it. What else could I do? I remember I used to day dream about running away and becoming a Major League Baseball player or a rock star. I had it all played out in my mind. But I knew even back then that it was only a dream.

My mom and dad didn't have any other children so I was it. It wasn't that bad though. I used to get all the attention from my relatives, and when my mom did get home from work or school all her attention was geared toward me. I remember we lived in these apartments in what now is considered probably one of the worst areas in Michigan. But back then it was okay. My mom really did her best to take care of me, and as a kid I couldn't have asked for too much more. I started getting

11

used to this whole divorce thing, and the way I understood life was just fine with me. I didn't want anything to change. I wanted it to stay just the way it was. But I guess that was wishful thinking because my mom introduced me to her new friend. Her new friend was more than just a friend, and soon he was coming around more and more. So now between work, school and my mom's boyfriend there was less and less time for me. Then things got pretty serious between them and I was introduced to his two kids. He had a boy and a girl, and his son was a kid who loved to get dirty and play in the dumpsters. I was the total opposite. My mom made sure I was clean and my clothes never had any dirt on them. Imagine what you might picture someone who attends Harvard University looking like and that would have been me. I remember hearing a story that my soon to be brother had me playing in a garbage dumpster, and my mom was freaking out because my white Winnie the Pooh pants were getting dirty. Not only was I being introduced to new things, I was also being introduced to a whole new way of life – a life that one day would prove to be my downfall.

My mom and her boyfriend decided that they were going to buy a house, and suddenly all in one shot I had a ready-made family. So off I went to play house with these new people in my life. My mom's boyfriend's kids lived with their mom so moving into this house was just us. You know the thing I hate about divorce is this. No one at any point ever sat me down and explained what was going on. I had to figure all this out on my own, and I didn't handle it well. One day I have a dad and the next I don't. One day it's just me and my mom and the next it's a whole family. I was old enough at the time for someone to say, "Hey Scott this is what's going on."

Communication goes a long way especially with kids; and when you uproot their lives it's pretty important! This new life that I was now living also included a new school, new friends, and a whole new city to learn. But I adapted pretty quickly, and I think for the most part I enjoyed it. My dad would pick me up every other Friday and drop me off at school on Monday morning. I also got to see him every Wednesday after school. I still saw my grandmas and aunts, but since I was in school full time I didn't need to have anyone watch me unless I was sick. As I got older I had a key to the house, so after school I would come home and be by myself until my mom or her new husband who was now my stepdad (they got married) would come home. All in all I was pretty much on my own. Not bad for a kid but with that kind of freedom, a kid will always find something to get into they shouldn't; and trust me I was no exception.

I am not too sure where I went wrong in life or even why, but I did. Maybe it was because of my parents' divorce, or maybe it was because all the attention that I once had was now being diverted to my new family. Whatever the case was it affected me greatly. My problems started off in school. As early as the second grade I was getting into trouble. My mom had me enrolled in a Catholic school and they had rules about dressing in uniforms and ties for the guys. I hated wearing ties; and even to this day I hate it because I have a problem with things around my neck. I feel like I am choking and I start to gag. One day I had my top button undone and my tie a little lose and the nun who was my teacher demanded that I button that top button and pull that tie up. I told her that it was too tight and that it made be gag, but she didn't care. She kept on demanding and I finally had enough so I told her to go screw herself. That was probably not a good thing for a second grader to tell a nun.

I started skipping school in the 4ᵗʰ grade and to this day I can't figure out for the life of me how I got away with it. I used to hustle the nuns all the time and tell them the day before I was going to skip that my grandmother had died and I wouldn't be there. They bought into this every time. I think my grandmother died like 10 times that year.

I remember I had this really nice lady for a principal. She was also a nun, but she was kind of cool and hip. I would literally be in her office everyday for something I pulled, but she also would listen to me and not just scream. Her discipline of me was always doing some type of office work. I would have to organize papers, lick envelopes, or carry desks and stuff from one room to the next. The next few years though started to get out of control, so out of control that I probably should have either won an Oscar award for performance or been locked up in juvenile prison.

Every day when I came home from school I had to call my mom and let her know I was home. Then I usually had to put the dinner she made in the oven so it would be done by dinner time. That was pretty much my life after school. One day though I was talking to my mom on the phone and I was standing by the new counter top my stepdad just put in the kitchen. Even till this day I have no idea why I did what I did; but I took a butcher knife out of the drawer and I started to cut up the end of the counter top. I kept on swinging it until it had notches all up and down the edges. Of course when they came home they saw it; but I lied and told them I had no idea how it happened.

14

After this incident, lying started to be like my second language. Actually it became my first language, because everything that came out of my mouth was a lie. When it came to school I would lie about everything. The school would mail progress reports to my house every couple of months; and I would get to the mail before my mom and would take them and put them in my drawer. Why I never threw them out is beyond me, because one time my mom went into my drawer and found about 20 of them. Other times teachers would call my mom and leave her a message on the answering machine at home to call them back. I would get to the answering machine before my mom, and I would erase the messages. My mom finally just gave the school her direct line to work and I couldn't get pass that.

Things got so bad that in the 8th grade my mom would literally sit in back of me in my classes and copy down what the teacher was saying and make me study it when I got home that day. Everyone including friends knew that Scott's mom didn't screw around. I changed my report card grades, I told teachers to go screw themselves and I threw stuff at teachers even while they were looking at me. I just didn't care, and I mean seriously didn't care. I didn't care if they threw me out or failed me. The funny thing though, was that every single teacher from the 5th grade to the 8th grade passed me. It wasn't because I deserved it. It was because I was so out of control that they didn't want me repeating their class or grade. I had one teacher who was an alcoholic, and I am pretty sure dealing with me on a day to day basis didn't help her addiction.

As I said earlier, lying was such a huge part of my life that there were times that I couldn't keep the lies straight. I think I started lying because I was looking for the attention that I used to get from my mom, and then it just turned into a habit thing. I would tell stupid lies too. I would have a friend who said they went to a baseball game and saw an all star hit a home run and I would say, "Oh yeah, well that guy is my cousin." People knew I was full of it, but they just dealt with it. I was a real loner when it came to friends. It was in part due to the lying and in part because I just wasn't cool. But I just enjoyed being by myself. Ironically, even though today I am a public speaker, I still just like to be by myself.

When I was a kid though, I missed out on a lot by being that way. One of the things that I used to do was collect baseball cards. I collected every card from every year, and it literally consumed my days. I couldn't wait for school to be over so I could go home and look at and inventory my cards. I actually hooked up my closet and turned it into my little baseball card office. I had a filing cabinet and a chair, and it was just big enough for me to sit in. Here's the funny thing about me. I never cracked a book in school except to throw towards a teacher. But it wasn't because I wasn't smart. It wasn't because I had a learning problem. It came down to the fact that it just didn't interest me. But when something interested me like baseball cards you couldn't get me away from learning. I used to study the back of baseball cards and know every stat about a certain player. I would know their RBI's, home runs, batting average and so on. Even to this day someone will bring up a player back from the 80's and be wrong about that players hit total for a certain year, and I will have to correct them. They look at me like I'm crazy. So learning wasn't the problem. It was just what I wanted to learn about. My freshmen year my mom asked me with all sincerity, "Scott please just try for one semester, do that for me please." So I did. When I got that report card for the semester I had a 3.5 grade point average. I don't think I cracked a book either but I paid attention in class. My stepdad tells a story that it used to piss him off because while everybody else needed to study hard to get a good grade, I would just listen and then take a test and get an A or a B. But once that semester was over so was I, and by the 10th grade the school had had enough and kicked me out. They actually called me into the principal's office and told me, "We tried to call your mom but there was no answer, so please pass this message on to her that you are not welcome back next year." My mom had to put down a deposit before the school year ended for the following year, and they handed me that check back and told me to give it to her. Yeah right, like I was going to do either one of those things. I took that check and filed it under, "I don't care" and went about my summer.

Well the new school year began and my mom wanted to know why I wasn't in school. After a very brief phone call to the principal of my old school she found out everything. She marched my butt straight into the public school and signed me up. It wasn't a very good day to say the least.

School was not the only trouble I was getting into and when my step-brother came to live with us I took my craziness to an all time high- for a young teen anyway. My step-brother moved into our house when I was about 10 years old. It was a little different at first because by this time I was already established in the house and I was used to being by myself; but none the less it was pretty cool to have a brother. My brother though liked to get into things a lot more than I would have ever gotten into on my own. One year for Christmas he and I received BB guns for a present. I think within about

17

three weeks people's garage windows started getting shot out. In the summer we would put our winter gear on and shoot each other. Around the 4th of July he and I would get a bunch of bottle rockets and shoot them at each other, never thinking we could kill each other or at least take an eye out. But we had fun.

Our fun turned into something serious though and if it were to happen today not only us but our parents would be in a world of trouble. We grew up in a decade where cars had these real cool hood ornaments on the front of them. Cadillac, Benz and Chrysler had some of the nicest ones. One day as we were walking back from the store we decided to steal one off a car. Well that one turned into two, and that two turned into 50 or so. We would collect them and use them as key rings. The ones we didn't use we put in a bag and threw them in the back of my closet so no one would find them. One day my stepdad had to go into my closet to do something and he came across the bag of hood ornaments. I'll never forget watching my brother walk up the driveway coming home from school and me trying to warn him to turn around and leave. He couldn't understand me and walked right into it. I remember my mom saying that we had to go return these to the places from which we stole them and apologize. But then I think my stepdad figured out we had done about $500 damage to each car and they would ending up paying for it if she made us do that, so that was the end of that conversation.

My brother and I always had chores to do growing up. We would trade off washing and drying dishes, but we also had to vacuum the whole house like every other day, wash the kitchen and bathroom floors, and cut and edge the grass about once a week. My stepdad owned his own electrical company, and if he worked on a Saturday he would take us with him. Now don't get me wrong, I now appreciate the way I grew up because I have values a lot of people don't, but my childhood also suffered from it. My friends got to watch cartoons on Saturday morning and play while I had to do something other than that. But also I got to travel to places like London, France, Amsterdam and Holland when my other friends would be up at the lake.

During one of those chore days my mom told us that we had to cut the grass in the back of our neighbor's garage because she was having a party and she didn't want the guests to see that mess. So my brother and I went back there and for some reason I decided instead of cutting it, I would throw some gas on it and light it up. Bad move. The grass went up quick. I thought it was hilarious, but my brother didn't. He ran into our house and got the fire extinguisher and put the fire out. Another minute or so and I probably would have been charged with arson because the garage would have been gone with God knows what else.

TWO

DARKNESS AND ADDICTION

There are a few things that I regret in life and wish I could do over. One is going to high school prom and the other is graduating and walking down the aisle. After I was kicked out of the Catholic high school, I had to attend a public high school and I probably would have come close to graduating. But like just about everything else in my life, this too would turn out badly. One day I was seriously sick during 4th period, and I went to the school office so they could call my mom to get permission to send me home. To tell this story I have to throw this in here. I started kindergarten a year before I had to and I ended up having to repeat it. So by the time my senior year started I was already 18 years old. Now back to the school office. The lady who was in charge of calling my mom looked at my school ID and said, "Scott you are an adult. We don't need to call your parents anymore. You are allowed to sign out whenever you want." Hearing those words was like hitting the lottery. It didn't take long for them to kick me out because I missed so much school. I would go in at 8:00am and sign out at 8:30. Needless to say, my mom never found out about me leaving every day until it was too late. She got the letter from the school before I did and she had enough of me. She called my dad and told him it was time for him to step up and take me in. She was throwing me out.

Moving to my dad's house was about the worst thing that could happen to me on so many different levels. First of all, my mom had never taken action as drastic as this, so the drive to my dad's house was filled with tears. I was wondering why she hated me so much. Obviously she didn't, but back then I sure felt like that. As I pulled up to my dad's house that afternoon I looked at my new house and said, "Man this blows. I don't want to be here anymore than they want me here." But I had no other choice. I had nowhere else to live.

The minute that I walked into the door my dad sat me down and gave me the house rules and what he expected of me. These rules were a little different than I had at my mom's house; but nevertheless they were rules and I had a problem following them. Just because I changed addresses doesn't mean I left all my problems at the old address though I think my parents were hoping that I would have.

My dad had two simple rules: get a job and start night school so I could finally graduate. My mom made me get jobs too when I lived with her, and what I mean by jobs is I probably worked at every place that was in my city at one time or another. I would either never show up or just quit. Or I would get fired. I had no work ethic to speak of and why my dad thought all of a sudden I did was beyond me, but he demanded it so off I went. The first thing I did was sign up for night school. The only good thing about that was the girl who worked in the office was a senior at that school and I started dating her. As far as the job went, it didn't. Here was the thing with me back then. I think getting into trouble and lying was like a game to me. I would go to extreme lengths to cover stuff up and not get caught, and telling my dad I had a job when I didn't was no exception.

21

I told my dad I was working at a shoe store by the mall. He had no reason to believe I was lying. But what I would do is sit in the parking lot by the store just in case my dad would come by to check up on me. Every day I would just sit there and listen to the radio for 8 hours a day. One day while sitting there I was about to leave and go to the store. Just as I was about to back out I saw my dad pull in. I was a very good liar and I was always quick with my responses. I got out of my car and started walking toward the shoe store and acted like I never saw my dad. He called my name and I turned around like I was surprised. I told him I just got back from lunch and had to go back to work. He never really thought anything of it and by seeing me there he would have never thought that I would sit out there like I did all day. So off he went thinking I had a job. That only bought a little bit of time though. I needed to start making some money and quick.

Night school was a joke. Now I am sure some people who attend night school actually get something out of it and graduate, but the only thing I got out of it was how to do lines of coke off a desk without getting caught by the teacher. Seriously think about this. Most people who attend night school couldn't cut it in a regular school, so the people that are there are not the greatest students. I was no exception. I was only going because I had to. I met a few different girls that were in my classes, and before I knew it I was busy partying with them at their houses and not going to school. I was introduced to a lot of crap during this period of my life. I was doing drugs like acid, mescaline and cocaine, and I started to drink pretty heavily. I was introduced to some real insane sexual things, and the people I was hanging out with were dabbling in the dark side of life- not a good combination for someone like me to get into. By nature I am compulsive, so no matter what I did if I liked it, I took it to the extreme. The drugs I was being introduced to took away all the pain I had. They made me feel like I was a brand new person inside and out. I think that is why I lied so much. When I lied I wasn't Scott. I could be whoever I wanted to be, and I was looking for that more than anything in my life. I wanted to be not me.

The sex was also another type of release for me. The sexual part of me was ruined when I was about 12. I had a cousin who would give me oral sex in exchange for money. I was basically being a male prostitute at a very young age. He was a few years older than me and I am pretty sure I had no idea what I was really getting myself into at the time but it is something that carried all the way through my adulthood. On top of being introduced to sex by the way of another man, I also got caught up in looking at XXX magazines. In order to get myself off with him I had to look at women performing sexual acts. I wasn't gay so I needed to see women having sex. Being introduced to women having sex in a magazine is just as bad if not worse than what I was doing with my cousin. In these magazines I saw women having sex with multiple men. I saw them having anal sex and I saw them getting abused and liking it, or at least so I thought. So here is the bottom line. I am a young teen, whose first sexual act was with another man, and whose first sexual encounter with a women was through a magazine and they were being abused. But I didn't know that they were being abused at the time, so I went through my teens and young adult years thinking this was how sex was supposed to be.

Eventually my dad got curious as to when I was going to get my first check from the job I didn't have. We had an agreement that I would pay him rent and start saving some money. I knew the time was coming that he would find out I was lying and probably kick me out. So one day while he was at work, I went through one of his drawers to see what I could get to maybe pawn. He had a drawer with a lot of stuff in it that I knew he never really looked in much. As I went through that drawer, I came across a check book that had to do with my grandpa's estate. My grandpa had died a year or so earlier, and my dad had a bank account set up from the estate sale. It wasn't a real lot of money but it did have a few thousand in the account. I sat back and thought about how I could write out those checks and cash them. As I said before, I only lived for the moment, so to speak, so I never really looked at what kind of consequences my actions would have. I took out one check from the account and I wrote it out to me. I remember driving to the bank thinking absolutely nothing. I didn't care. I didn't think. When I got to the teller it hit me that if I got caught doing this my ass would be in a world of trouble. I handed the check to the teller along with my driver's license, and she looked at the check and took it to the back of the bank. I thought, "Oh man, I'm busted." What she did with that check (that I had no idea they did) was match up the signature on the check with the signature on what they call a signature card. It's a card that a person signs in front of a manager or teller when they open an account. They know that the signature card is real, so if it doesn't match the check then they call the cops.

The second thing that I did know but I guess I just didn't care was that I was using my real driver's license. Even if this worked, eventually my dad would find out someone ripped off his account because all they would have to do was go back and look to see who cashed the check. I wasn't the smartest criminal at the time. The teller came back with a crazy look on her face. She said, "Is this your dad's checking account?" I said, "Well kind of..." and I told her about my grandpa. She said, "Oh now I see, that makes sense. We had two different names on the account and wanted to make sure that was right." She asked me if I would like to be put on the account also. That way you could cash checks without having to go through all this every time I came in. "Um, okay," was all I could say. These people literally just handed me a blank check and said go ahead. I started cashing checks every few days. If I ran out of money I would just go and cash a check. It was pretty simple or so I thought. I had to have known that the day would come when my dad would find out, and that day turned out to be just right around the corner.

With the money I stole, I started to shoot pool at the local pool hall. I always loved to shoot and over time I became pretty good at it. I loved playing nine ball. It's a quick moving game that you can either make a lot of money betting on or lose a lot depending on how lucky you were. Hanging out at a pool hall is probably not the smartest thing to do if you are looking to stay out of trouble, but it became my second home. I made a few friends there; and I took my partying to a whole new level. I was only 19 at the time and my friends were over 21, but that didn't matter because one of my friends looked like my twin. He gave me an older driver's license he had, and that ID allowed me to go bar hopping and buy liquor whenever I wanted. No one ever questioned it. Needless to say my drinking started to become a problem. I wouldn't drink during the day because my dad thought I was working, but the minute I came home and went out I needed a drink. I was quickly, not slowly, becoming an alcoholic. Plus all the drugs I was doing made it seem like I was never drunk. When you get high off coke and pot, the buzz from the alcohol takes a back seat so you begin to drink more than you should. There are no limits. You don't know that you are drunk.

But I knew it was becoming a serious issue, because one day I was at my aunt's house on Christmas Eve and I started to shake a little bit. I had this edge to me that was getting worse by the minute. I forgot the fake ID I used at my dad's house, so I couldn't go to a store and buy. And besides, it was Christmas Eve. Who is going to leave their families to go buy for me? Once I did find someone, it was too late. You couldn't buy alcohol past 9:00PM on Christmas Eve. I needed something. I needed a drink because it was getting bad. So when everyone went upstairs at my aunt's house, I stayed downstairs and started going through her cabinets. I looked in every cabinet and the only thing I could find was slow Gin. Slow Gin is used primarily for cooking, but I didn't care. It had something like 18% alcohol in it so I drank it. It tasted like I was drinking motor oil, but it served its purpose for that night. I never knew how to reach out for help in those days, but there was many a day that if my dad would have been paying attention, he would have known I needed it.

Three

MY ONLY ESCAPE

"Scott, get your ass out of that bed. Someone stole the money from my dad's bank account and I bet it was one of your friends that did it." That was how I found out that the bank had finally called my dad to tell them they were closing the account because all the money had been withdrawn. I told my dad I was not sure what had happened to the money and if it was one of my friends, I had no idea. I think the only thing that saved me that day from getting killed and my dad ending up in prison for a very long time was that he had to go back to work, and the bank was still looking into the matter. When he left I started packing. I knew that by that afternoon they would have figured out it was me and that would be it. I had nowhere to go. I had no money left. So before I left I went into my dad's room one last time and stole his hand gun, figuring I could at least sell it while I figured out what I was going to do next. I grabbed all my stuff, threw it into the car, and drove out of the driveway. I remember thinking as I was pulling out that I probably would never see my dad again; and that was about as hard for me to think about as getting kicked out of my mom's house. But in the mean time I needed to think and I needed alcohol. Off to the liquor store I went.

That day turned into night real quick. I drove around all day thinking, "What the hell am I supposed to do now?" and here it was night already. I had enough money to buy three, 40

27

ounce beers, which is the equivalent of about 10 beers. I parked in the school parking lot across the street from my ex-girlfriend's house. It was raining and snowing outside and I had nowhere to go, so I just sat there drinking. Here is the problem with drinking when you are already depressed. Alcohol is a downer and when you combine that with the problems you are having, the problems seem to get a lot worse than what they are. Now my problems didn't need any help to get worse, but the more I drank the more it seemed like I was so screwed.

I started thinking about the cops who were probably looking for me now. I thought about my dad out looking for me, and it wasn't to bring me home. Every car that drove past I thought was the cops or my dad, and the more I drank the worse it got. Then it hit me. Something told me, "Hey idiot, you have that hand gun in the back seat. That will solve all your problems." I thought, "Oh yeah, I totally forgot about that." So I reached back there, grabbed the gun, and placed it on my lap. For the next hour I would take a sip of my beer and look at the gun, take a sip and look at the gun. Finally I grabbed the gun and I raised it towards my mouth. I remember shaking so bad and to this day I don't know if it was because I was cold, drunk, or just scared that this would be my last moment on earth. I thought about how my mom and dad would react to the news that their kid just blew his head off in a school parking lot. And I thought about who would find me. I hoped it would be my ex-girlfriend.

I put the barrel in my mouth and I closed my eyes. This was it. No more trouble, no more houses to get kicked out of, and no more addictions. As I pulled the trigger I heard a sound I will never forget as long as I live, a sound that I am so grateful for today. The sound I heard was a click. The gun never went off. The bullet never left the chamber. I pulled the barrel out and just sat there and looked at the gun. I opened the chamber. I looked to see if there were bullets. There were. There were six of them. "What the heck?" I thought. "I can't even kill myself." I threw the gun in the back of the car and sat there for a minute.

Then I remembered a story I had seen in high school about two teens who had killed themselves by stuffing a shirt into the tail pipe of their running car. They died from carbon monoxide poisoning. So I reached in my bag and I grabbed the first shirt I could get my hands on. I was serious about this so I had no time to coordinate what shirt I was going to shove in the tail pipe. I got out of the car and shoved that shirt as far as I could up the tail pipe and got back in to finish my beer. After about 45 minutes of absolutely nothing but a bad headache I gave up. What I didn't know back then was the car couldn't be parked outside like mine was because the carbon monoxide would escape into the air and not fill up the car. The headache I got was from some of the fumes that leaked back into the car but that was about it.

"Now what?" I thought. I had no other options. My only option was to die and when that didn't happen I needed a place to stay, I needed a shower, I needed to lay my head down and just sleep. Maybe when I woke up this would all be a dream. I had many thoughts running through my head but none of them were good. This gun that I couldn't kill myself with was going to be my way to make money. I had never robbed anybody with a gun, but I never have been in a situation like this before either. So I started plotting, "Who can I jack?" At one point I was seriously thinking about robbing the bank that got me into this predicament, but I was too scared to do anything like that; so I went to a friend of mine and asked him if I could crash at his house for a few days. I said this before and I'll say it again. Hanging out at a pool hall was not a place to be if you're trying to stay out of trouble. I wish I would have had these thoughts back then because the friend I ended up staying with was way more trouble than I could handle. Little did I know it then but these next few days would kick start my criminal career into motion and it wouldn't stop until a decade later.

Four
MOST WANTED PART I

The house I was crashing at belonged to a friend that I met while shooting pool a few months earlier. I had no idea what he was into besides partying, but I was about to find out first hand. The first night I was there he asked me if I wanted to make some quick cash. Of course I did so I said, "Yeah sure what do I have to do?" This guy and a few others would go out every night and steal parts off cars at dealerships. Then they would sell them back to whomever was requesting the order that day. My job was easy that first night. I was hired to be the look out. I had to stand at the front of the dealership and warn everyone else if the cops where coming. That night went perfectly. No problems, no cops, and a few hundred dollars in my pocket. I thought to myself, "Man this is good living. A few hundred dollars every night just to stand around. I could get used to this." But my few hundred dollars a night was about to end and my future held something quite different than living on someone's floor. I was about to live the life I always wanted. The life of a rock star or so I thought.

One of the nights that we all went out to steal was a bonus day for me. I was promoted from being a look out to actually stealing car parts. This particular night we were hitting a pretty big dealership and our orders where to get all the car stereos that had tape players in them. We would either bust out the windows using the ceramic from a spark plug (ceramic will

31

shatter a window without breaking it into a thousand pieces) or we would break the door locks and get in that way. When we would go out and steal it would always be sometime between midnight and 3:00 AM. We wanted to make sure that most people would be sleeping and not on the road in the middle of the night. Less chance to get caught or so we thought.

This particular night we broke into and stole 26 car stereos. We had a van that we used. That way, if we had a lot of parts we could just throw them in the back. We loaded up the van with the stereos and headed out of the parking lot. Within about 10 seconds of leaving the parking lot we were pulled over by about 20 police officers. I'm not sure if you know what it's like to get arrested by a swat team, but I can tell you from the couple of times I have that it is not a pleasant experience. They pulled us out of the van by whatever they could grab, and they pointed automatic weapons at our heads. They were screaming at us about not listening, and they told us they would blow our "freaking" heads off if we made any sudden moves. I had only seen stuff like this in movies and on TV. Now I was living it. They handcuffed us and threw us in back of the police cars. Off to the jail we went. I will never forget the ride to the jail. I had no idea how much trouble I was in. I thought they had the death penalty for crimes like this. I didn't know any better. Off to court I went.

The judge spoke loud and clear. "How do you plead, Mr. Mason?" My lawyer, whom I had just met like 5 seconds before, leaned over and told me to say not guilty. "Not guilty your honor," I said. "Fine, your bond will be $50,000 cash. Your next court date will be in 14 days." I looked at my lawyer and said, "I don't have $50,000 to get out." He said,

"Then I will see you in 14 days." This was my first time in jail, and I had no chance of getting out for at least 14 days. My lawyer said, "Don't worry, the county jail isn't that bad," and he left. Man was he wrong. Those 14 days were like hell or at least at the time that's what I thought. Little did I know in another year or so I would be heading to a place that made the county jail look like a camp for kids.

The next court date I had, the judge allowed me to go home. But where was home? I knew my dad wasn't going to take me back in, and my mom sure wasn't going to, so I was kind of screwed here. The judge made it clear that before he would let me out I needed someone to take me in. So my aunt and uncle came to my rescue and said I could live with them. I guess they felt bad for me and maybe they thought I deserved a second chance. Either way I was grateful because I had had enough of that county jail. So off I went. This would be my third family in less than one year and nothing changed except my address. Well check that, one thing did change. I became crazier as the time went on and there was nothing anyone could have done for me except get out of the way.

My aunt and uncle had a few rules for me when I got to their house. One was I had to get a job and pay them rent. For some reason this time it hit me that I really had to get a job. I was able to get one at a grocery store working midnights. I would stock the selves. I became pretty good at it and I made a few friends. Things were going pretty good for me for awhile. I had a job, I had a new girlfriend and I was almost happy. I say almost, because at this time my dad still wouldn't talk to me and I really didn't see my mom too much. Even though I really had no regard for anyone but myself, I still missed my mom and dad. But life had to go on. My cousin who I was living with worked at a fast food place down the street from us, so I decided to get a second job. Here I wouldn't have worked for the life of me a few months ago, and now I have two jobs. Like I said things were really starting to go in the right direction for me. I seriously felt good about myself. I wasn't too sure where I was going, but I knew that if I kept this up the sky was the limit.

On one of my days off, my aunt asked me if I would clean out the basement closet and get it organized. I was good at cleaning because my mom had me doing it since I was a little kid, so I didn't mind. Besides I loved to listen to music while I cleaned. It was kind of like a drug for me. It helped me escape my problems for a little while. When I was a kid I would put on rock concerts, and I used to dream about being on a stage every single day of my life. Maybe that was God's way of putting in my heart what I would be doing later on in life- being on a stage in front of thousands of people and loving every moment of it. But that wasn't the plan for this day. This day I was putting on a show for a mop and broom. As I started to move boxes out I came across one that said company checks. I opened the box and sure enough, there were stacks upon stacks of company checks not made out to anyone. My uncle owned a company that installed cable lines throughout the U.S. and these checks were left over from when the business failed. The moment I found these checks, everything I had worked for up to this point went straight out the window. I instantly knew that I could probably cash these checks anywhere since they were payroll checks; and I knew just the place to cash them.

The next morning I grabbed one of these checks and wrote it out to me for $450. Just like when I stole my dad's checks, I

34

didn't care that I was going to get caught. I just wanted the money and wanted the high of doing it. I am somewhat of an adrenalin junky. I love the idea of sky diving, cliff jumping, going speeds in cars that most people wouldn't even consider and so on. I think a lot of the crimes that I committed were because I needed that adrenalin high. I took that check to the grocery store where I was working and asked them if they would cash my payroll check. First of all I worked there, so they never even considered that this was a stolen check. Secondly, the manager of the store lived a few houses away from my aunt so he never questioned it. After they cashed that check, I remember going out and buying a bag of pot and then going down to my girlfriend's house to get high with her dad. That was probably the only day he and I ever got along. There would be times down the road that he tried to kill me, and I don't mean figuratively. But that night we got stoned.

I started cashing checks once a week, but then I figured out I could cash two a week by using different managers. When one manager was off I would use the other one and so on. I started to get about $800 a week total on top of what I was making working nights there. Till this day I am not sure what I spent all that money on, but I am sure it was a lot of drugs and alcohol. I went back to my old ways real quick, and in keeping with the theme of my old ways, I was about to get caught once again. But this wasn't my parents I was ripping off, it was a major company, and the consequences were to be a little different than mom and dad being mad at me. I found out that I had been caught when one of the managers of the store came knocking on my aunt's door one morning. I will never forget her screaming at me from upstairs, "What did you do? What did you do?" over and over again. I seriously had no idea until

I walked up stairs and saw the checks sitting there on the table. I was busted.

Now I've got to give it to my aunt. She didn't call the cops on me, and she talked the manager into giving her a few days to figure all this out before he called the police to press charges for embezzlement. My aunt sat me down at the table and handed me a cigarette and said, "Alright, how are we going to get you out of this?" Here I'm thinking I'm going to jail and she is trying to keep me out. My uncle on the other hand wasn't so nice. He wanted me out of the house and he wasn't taking "no" for an answer. But my aunt came up with a plan to buy me a few days. She drove me down to the local hospital and just before we went in, she told me to tell them at the desk that I was suicidal. They would have to put me in the psychiatric ward for at least 72 hours, and then from there we would figure it out.

Now this wasn't my first trip to this ward. Back when I was 18 and a senior, I told the counselor at school that I took a bottle of aspirin; and they called an ambulance. After about three hours in the E.R. and them making me drink this charcoal crap to throw up, they figured out that I was lying and they put me in the psych ward for 72 hours. Basically I have been down this road before, so I knew what to say and not to say. They admitted me on a 72 hour suicidal stay and off I went. I have no idea what transpired after that, but somehow my mom got involved and made a deal with the grocery store. If they didn't prosecute me, she would pay the money back. Once again I was off the hook, and once again it wouldn't take long for me to start screwing up. Only this time I wouldn't have my mom by my side. Actually I wouldn't have anyone by my side but me.

Maybe you haven't figured this out yet, but I wasn't a very good criminal. I pretty much got caught at whatever I did because I just didn't care. Someone asked me once how much money I stole over my criminal career. With all the cars and stuff it's well into the hundreds of thousands. But it's not like I took a bunch of money and went to a stock broker and said, "Here invest this." If I had $100 or $1,000, you can bet at the end of the day it would be gone. I would buy clothes, shoes, or jewelry. I even had hair extensions put in my hair to look cool and that cost some money. But like I said before, I wanted to live the life of a rock star so bad that I would have done anything to get that chance. Well anything came a knocking and I answered it.

Somehow I managed to get a job working the midnight shift at a hotel. I worked by myself and I could pretty much do whatever I wanted. This particular motel was used by hookers and drug addicts, so it wasn't the classiest place to be. One night I was working was busier than usual, and I took in a large amount of cash. I always had to put the cash in a drop safe and at the end of my shift I would write down what I took in that night. Then the manager would come in and count the day's cash and receipts. When I left that morning, I never dropped the money into the safe. I put it straight into my pocket and left. When the manager came in that morning she knew I had stolen the money and she called the police. But I was long gone by then, and I was on my way to playing rock star for one spectacular night. After I left the hotel, I went straight to the mall to buy some new clothes, shoes and jewelry. I figured if I was going to party, I was going to do it in style. When I was done there, I went to one of the most expensive hotels around and rented a room. I was ready for one spectacular night, and all I had to do now was call up a bunch of friends and invite them to the party of the year. I had one more crime to commit first though, and I was always looking for the opportunity. Opportunity came a knocking. And once again it was in a place I never would have thought.

I had to go to the desk to this swank hotel to ask a few questions about my new $500 a night room. There was a gentleman in front of me from Germany, so I had to wait my turn. I say that, because I thought the rich never had to wait in line for anything. As this guy was checking into the hotel, a bell boy came over and grabbed his suit cases and brief case and put them on a cart to take them upstairs. The bellboy put the cart in a room off to the side until the person who worked the floors came down to get them and deliver them to this guy's room. After this gentleman left and went up towards his room, I went into the room where his stuff was, stole his brief case, and took it to my room. Back then I don't think they had cameras like they do now, because if they did, I would have been busted a lot quicker than I was. I sat on my bed with the brief case trying to open it and because it was locked I couldn't get it open. I needed a screw driver or something to open the brief case and it's not like I had one in my back pocket. So I went down to the front desk and asked them if they had one. I told them I needed to fix my suitcase. On my way up to my room I must have had a million things running through my mind. I had no idea what was in this case but unless this guy was a thief like me, I assumed he must be rich. I finally got to my room and got the brief case open. I went through every inch of that brief case and I found absolutely nothing. I did find some currency from another country but that wasn't going to do me any good. And I did find credit cards, a driver's license, checking account information, a Social Security card, and things like that, but no money.

I remember sitting back on that bed and thinking about how I could use all this stuff to get money. I knew I couldn't use the credit cards because they would ask for I.D., so that was out. Then I wondered if there was a way that I could use the credit cards at an ATM machine, but I had no way of knowing his pin number. Then it hit me. I could try and change his pin number by calling the credit card company and give them the performance of a life time. And I did just that. I took all the information that I had on the guy and went across the street from the hotel to put my plan in action.

I didn't want to use the hotel room phone, so I went to a pay phone in a building across the street from the hotel. This was one of the rare moments I actually cared about getting caught. I was always pretty cool, calm and collective when stealing things. There were times that I would walk into a major department store, get what I wanted, and walk right out without paying. Other times I would walk in and take something off the shelf and go right to the return desk without even leaving and return what I had just stolen. And the crazy thing is, they never questioned me. They not only returned the item but gave me cash back.

Well, calling the credit card company needed to be one of those cool and collected moments. As I said, I needed to put on a performance of a lifetime. I called the 800 number on the back of the card, and I got a lady who sounded like she was really bitchy so I hung up. I needed the right person so I called back. The lady on the other end of the phone sounded real sweet, and I started to give her this line of crap that I was divorcing my wife and I needed to change the pin number on my credit card. She was real polite and had no idea that I wasn't who I said I was. She asked me all these security questions and I answered everyone because I had all his information in front of me from his brief case. Towards the end of our conversation she had one more question, and the answer to this question could not be found in the brief case. As a matter of fact it was a question that only the card holder would know the answer to. She asked me where was the last place I used the card to make a purchase. She wanted to know the city and what the purchase was. I thought, "Are you kidding?!" Here this lady sounds so sweet and now she is killing me.

How would I know this answer? I thought for a second and gave this a shot. I told her that I used the card at a certain hotel in a certain city about two hours ago. I figured he used his credit card at the hotel, and I figured right. She asked me what I would like my new pin number to be and I was in! I stole a lot of money that day and you would think that with what I just pulled off, I wouldn't let a little thing like a pager get me caught. But I did. And for you out there that don't remember what a pager is, it is a device that you could call and it would display a phone number for you to call that person. Back then it was the thing to have.

The next day I was heading to Augusta, Georgia to go live with my aunt or at least hang out for awhile. I needed out of the state in which I was living. I had cops trying to put me in prison and it had almost become a full time job to them to keep up with me. The crimes I was committing where getting out of hand. Every day I tried a new one that got me deeper and deeper into trouble. I figured if I got out and had a change of scenery it might change who I was becoming. That morning

I went down to the front desk and asked them to take me to the airport. They had a service that would drive you anywhere you wanted to go. I actually used this service the night before to go to all the ATM machines in the area to get the money from this credit card I had stolen. After about the 5th one the driver got suspicious, so I had to give him a couple hundred dollars to keep it between us. Funny how money will buy almost anything! Well, while I was at the desk requesting a ride, the manager was asking me a whole lot of questions about where I was going etc. I guess I never really thought too much about it. and just chalked it up as being polite. But little did I know the cops where on their way.

The hotel did everything they could to keep me there, but off I went to the airport. When I got there I checked my luggage in and proceeded to the gate from which my flight was to leave in about an hour. I had a duffle bag with some clothes and a whole lot of money that I was taking that with me on the flight. As I sat down I start looking for my pager. I went through the duffle bag, I went through my pockets. I looked everywhere. Then I remembered I left it in the hotel's car. So I called the hotel to ask them to get a hold of my driver so he could come back and drop off the pager to me. This was a stupid move on my part. They asked me what airline I would be at and they told me to just hang tight while they got a hold of him.

I started to walk through the airport towards the exit so I could meet him out there. I was hoping I wouldn't miss my flight because of this stupid pager. As I headed towards the door, I was met by I'm not sure how many, but a whole lot of sheriff officers with their guns drawn on me. It was a repeat of the last few years of my life. One cop was yelling at me to get

41

on the ground, while another grabbed me and threw me face down onto the concrete floor and handcuffed me. When they finally lifted me off the ground, I looked around at all the startled faces of all those people that were there in the airport when I got arrested. I'm sure I was the talk of many dinner conversations that night.

I spent 14 days in the county jail for that incident. They let me out on bond because the county jail was overcrowded. You would think that all these crimes I had committed up to this point would have gotten me a 20 year sentence; but for some reason they just kept on either putting me on probation or they would just let me out because of overcrowding. I remember I had a conversation with this older black guy who was in the county jail with me. He told me that if I continued on down the path I was going that eventually they would send me to prison. And he also told me about how prison life was. He had spent many years there and he was headed back himself. He really tried to get through to me though. The last words he told me were, "Scott you do not want to end up in Jackson prison." I just looked at him and said, "I will never go to prison."

Five

WE AREN'T IN KANSAS ANYMORE

It was 1992 and I was headed to Jackson State Prison. As the van pulled up to this crazy looking fortress, I looked at the guy who was shackled to me and thought about what I told that guy in the county jail. "I will never go to prison." Not only was I headed to prison, but I was shackled to one of Michigan's most notorious serial killers, Leslie Allen Williams. This guy raped, killed and kidnapped something like 13 girls. He was headed back to prison for life; and I was shackled to him. I had literally just turned 21 when I was sentenced for stealing a car, so that entitled me to end up in the "Big House"- Jackson State Penitentiary. At the time it was the largest walled prison in the world. All the stories I had heard about this place never captured how this place really looked or what it smelled like. It had this eerie darkness to it. I had seen a rundown haunted castle in Amsterdam when I was a kid, and this looked just like it. The front of this place just went on and on, and there were guards on the roof with M-14's, watching us as we got out of the van. They warned us that if we tried to escape we would be shot on site. I didn't know about anyone else, but escape was the last thing on my mind. I was thinking about all the stories I heard about prison and this particular one for sure. I had heard about rape, murder, and stabbings. I had heard that if you can't fight or stab someone, you will become their bitch (prison wife). I had heard stories that once you go to prison it's hard to get out; and if they do let you out, the other inmates become jealous and they try to kill you. All those stories I had heard were running through my mind. I didn't know what to think, and I sure didn't know what to do. But the correction officers sure did, and they weren't shy about telling you.

When I first walked into this prison I thought to myself, "This isn't too bad... nothing like I imagined." But I was wrong. I was in this room for about 5 minutes, and they had everyone strip down to absolutely nothing. Here I was standing next to 20 other guys butt naked. One by one we went into this shower area where they made us scrub down. And when we were done, they threw this white delousing powder all over us. I found out later that it was to kill lice if we had it. From that point we all had to get our new clothes-two blue shirts, two blue pairs of pants, under wear, socks, and a black pair of shoes. They really didn't care what size you were. They just guessed. I was lucky though, because everything they gave me fit.

From that point I had to go get my picture taken for my state ID. This ID had to be carried by me at all times throughout my prison stay. From there I headed over to this area where a lady behind this counter asked me a lot of questions and told me about my prison sentence. She told me what I already knew. I was sentenced to 2-5 years for one count of auto theft out of Oakland County, Michigan. And because I had warrants out for my arrest in other counties as well; they needed to put me in a higher class of security until those were taken care of. The warrants that I had were for not showing up to court for that credit card fraud I pulled back at the hotel. I also had one count of conspiracy for breaking and entering an auto with damage. And I had 26 counts for breaking and entering an auto with damage that was from back when I left my dad's house. They had put me on probation with the stipulation if I got in trouble again within 2 years they could charge me, and they did just that. The conspiracy charge was because they considered me to be a part of a Theft Ring.

The prosecuting attorney that was handling our cases was running for some type of office; and he was going to make sure that everyone knew that his office stopped the auto thief bandits. So he charged all of us with this conspiracy charge, which by the way is very serious. When they start to classify you with charges like that, if they proceed to convict you, your sentence doubles. So let's say I got 5 years for the 26 counts of breaking and entering an auto with damage. Well because of that conspiracy charge it now increases to 10 years in prison. Also it follows you for the rest of your life. The lady also told me that I would be going back and forth from prison to court to be tried on all these other counts, and my first court date was already set for later on that year. She smiled at me and said, "You know you don't look like you belong here. My advice to you is to get your life straight while you're here and stay out of trouble." Easier said than done.

Settling into my new prison life didn't take long. You really don't have a choice. You figured out quickly where the chow hall was and at what time food was served, because if you didn't go you would starve until the next meal. Not that it was such a bad thing to miss a meal. The food was absolutely disgusting. You figured out quickly what certain bells and horns where. The bells and horns are what ran your day. A certain bell would mean go to your cell for lockdown and another would mean it's yard time or chow time. But you couldn't ever miss those bells, because if you weren't where you were supposed to be then you would end up in a lot of trouble.

I also learned quickly who to trust and who not to trust. This would be hard at times though, because just when you thought someone was trying to be your friend they were actually trying to have sex with you. Homosexuality ran rampant throughout the prison system. I have seen many times over the years how guys who come into prison for the very first time get tested. Getting tested meant that someone would come up to you and tell you that if you didn't give up that ass then they were going to take it. Other times the test might be about money. If a certain gang knew you had a family on the outside who was supportive of you, they might try to extort you and your family. They would tell someone that they needed to pay for protection and if they didn't, they would either get stabbed or raped. Most times if the inmate fought back they would just leave them alone. But there were too many that were scared to fight; and they would have paid anything to be protected.

As I said homosexuality was a big part of prison culture. A lot of guys were doing 20 or 30 year prison sentences and they needed a way to have sex, even if it was with another man. The funny thing about some of these guys though was the minute they got out of prison, they would never even think about having sex with another man. They weren't gay. They just adapted to their surroundings. I know that sounds crazy but that's just the way it was. We classified homosexuals into two groups in prison. One was the closet queers. The ones who were sucking dick behind closed doors. And the other group were the flamers. The flamers acted like women, talked like women, and tried to dress like women by pulling up their pant legs or putting a knot on the bottom of their shirt. And they would wear makeup. I will get into how they got make up inside prison a little later, but I will tell you there wasn't anything you couldn't get while in prison. There also was another group of people that were treated like homosexuals, and that was the child molesters. Even if they weren't gay, they still had to perform sex acts with other men just to stay alive. The whole prison population for the most part hated child molesters, and if they didn't have a boyfriend protecting them then they were in trouble.

There were other groups inside prison, and these groups were the ones who ran the day to day operations of prison life, from the inmate standpoint anyway. The prison system across the board is generally run by gangs. Gangs in the prison system are basically classified by what race they are. Blacks, Whites, and Mexicans make up about 99% of prisons gangs in Michigan. Most of the gangs are nationally known gangs such as the Vice Lords, Latin Kings, Gangster Disciples, Mexican Mafia, Crips, Bloods and the Aryan Brotherhood. And out of those groups, there were smaller gangs that went by what side of a certain city you were from, or what street you were from. Gangs run in numbers, and the more people each gang had the more power they had. So each gang did everything they could to recruit a person when they first entered the prison system and I was no exception.

As I said earlier, homosexuality runs rampant inside the American prison system and Michigan was no different. I had to watch my back the first couple of weeks I was locked up (meaning I had to be aware of what was going on so I didn't get pulled into a cell or bathroom and get raped). Yeah, it was that serious. One of the most vulnerable places for something like this to happen would be the shower area. The shower room, depending on what prison you were in, had anywhere from 8-20 shower stalls in one area. So you could possibly be taking a shower with 19 other guys. I am sure you have heard people joke when showering in a public area, "Don't drop the soap." Well that joke is very real inside prison. If you drop your soap you just leave it on the ground and move on. I don't care if you just got into the shower and you drop it. You take a shower tomorrow with a new bar. You start bending over around 19 other guys and you are asking for trouble.

One day I had just finished taking a shower and I was brushing my teeth when a black guy in his 50's decided that he was going to grab my buttocks and wink at me. This guy was every bit of 350 pounds, and I knew if I was going to fight this guy it was not going to turn out good. But before I could say or do anything, he left. That's how these guys work. We called them predators and that is a perfect name for them. They prey on the weak. They prey on the ones they think they can get over on and this guy obviously thought that he could get over on me.

As I headed back to my cell it didn't take long for the word to get out that this guy had done this to me. The crazy thing about prison is if a guy gets stabbed in let's say cell block 5 and you are in cell block 1, the person in cell block 1 will know about that stabbing before the knife even hits the floor. Nothing is a secret and what had happened to me was no exception. As we locked down for count that afternoon I started to think about what I was going to do. I didn't have to be in prison for very long to know I had to take care of this in a violent matter. One of my favorite sayings I had heard since

I was a little kid was about being, "in a catch 22," and I was now living that saying. If I didn't take care of doing something to this guy, then I would be labeled a bitch and probably would be forced to have sex with men the rest of my time in prison. If I did take care of this guy in a violent matter, I risked going to the hole or getting a longer sentence for attempted murder or maybe even murder.

My neighbor, the guy that locked next to me was this 5'4" white guy that they called Shorty. Shorty was a member of a violent white supremacy gang and he hated black people, Mexicans, Jews and basically anyone who wasn't White. I learned after a few years of knowing Shorty that his size didn't really matter. People respected him as if he were 6'8" and 300 pounds. He was what we called, "off the hook crazy." He had no problem sticking a knife into you and eating a sandwich while doing it. Well Shorty got wind of what happened to me and he told me what he thought I should do. "You need to kill that nigger", Shorty said. "Great," I thought. "Now if I don't kill him then I have the whole white race wanting to come after me too." I told him I would do what I had to do, but I had no weapon to do it with and that he was too big for me to fight without a weapon. That day Shorty gave me a crash course in weapon training, penitentiary style. He proceeded to show me that the pad lock I used to lock my foot locker and two pairs of socks was all I needed. "You take the socks and double them up," Shorty said with a smile on his face. "And then you put the pad lock into the socks and tie the socks at the top into a knot. Make it tight," he said, 'you don't want the lock coming out when you are beating his fat black ass."

This was the first time I really ever witnessed racism in a violent way. I grew up five minutes away from Detroit, and I went to school with a lot of black people. I had good friends who were black, and now everything had to change and not by choice. I had to look at black people as the enemy. Shorty told me, "Tomorrow morning when you get to the shower, make sure you take that weapon and put it in your towel. And if he tries anything just start swinging until he falls. Don't let him get back up. Kill him if you have to. It's the only way."

I don't think that I slept that whole night. Shorty's words kept on swirling through my mind. "Kill him if you have to." The next day I went to take a shower after playing baseball on the yard. I think everyone but the guy who I was after knew that there was going to be a fight. As I got out of the shower I looked over to my right and there he was. I got my towel and dried off. The other towel had my weapon in it. I didn't want to start a fight if he wasn't going to do anything so I just waited. Just like the day before I started to brush my teeth, and then it happened. He went to go grab my ass and I grabbed my weapon and did everything I had been taught. Well almost everything. I didn't kill him, but I hit him enough times that he never messed with me again. But something greater happened that day. I got respect not only from the whites but also everyone else. Even if I would have got my ass kicked by this guy I still would of got respect, because I stood up for myself. My prison experience was about to change, but not for the better. I grew up wanting to be a gangster. I listened to gangster rap music, and I always watched the gangster movies on TV. But not in a million years would I have ever thought that one day I would be one of those gangsters.

SIX

DEALING INSIDE

When you enter the prison system you check a lot of things at the door. But how you acted on the outside is not one of those things. You do learn quickly though that if you were a loud mouth instigator on the outside, you probably need to change that or someone will do it for you. But I am talking more about addictions, whether it be drug addictions or personality addictions. Most inmates that come through the prison system are addicts of some sort, mostly drugs and alcohol. I think a lot of people believe that if someone goes to prison that once they are there, they will get clean, and be able to come out drug free. I wish that was the case because then a lot of people would be clean when coming home. But the fact of the matter is that I saw just as many drugs in prison as I did on the outside. There was a time for about a year that I smoked pot every day. How drugs get into prison isn't important, but what is important is what happens when they do get in there.

I always knew when a big drug shipment was coming into the prison. People started getting stabbed left and right or beat down. The violence almost tripled because guys would get drugs on credit and then never pay the dealer. I was no exception. I was addicted to coke and almost any drug that got me high before going to prison, but I never had the urge to do that while locked up. But I did like to smoke pot.

51

One day a big shipment of pot came in, and I was first in line to get some. We didn't have scales in prison to weigh drugs out on so we used Chap Stick lids to do our weighing. I know it sounds crazy right? A Chap Stick lid full of weed, which is not a lot, went for $25.00. If you bought 3 at $75.00 you got the fourth one free. What would happen is the dealer would give you what you wanted and then give you an address to where you would send the money. For example, if I had a girlfriend or wife when I got locked up, I would call her and tell her to send a $75.00 money order to such and such address, and that's how dealers would get paid. A lot of times the dealer would give you half up front, and when his contact got the money on the outside you would then get the other half. I was able to get something like $50.00 worth of pot on credit and I told the guy I would have the money sent. The problem was I had no body on the outside to send the money and I knew that. After about 3 weeks of me putting him off, he finally had enough. One day while I was walking to the yard he come up in back of me and punched me on the side of my head. He told me that was my payment. Years later I would run into this guy's uncle at another prison, and he and I became best friends. He got a letter one day from his nephew and it said, "Tell Scott hi and no hard feelings."

As I said earlier though, besides my drug addictions I had another addiction, and that was lying. And I could simply be myself around people. Now this got me into a lot of trouble in the world, but in the world I could always just run and hide. In prison there wasn't anywhere to run.

Before coming to prison I was dating a girl who was good friends with a cousin of mine. Her mom actually called the police on me for driving a stolen car. I had stolen a $40,000

Mark VIII and she knew that I didn't own that car so she called. That was actually the car that got me sent to prison. (Well that, and everything else I did.) One day this girl was visiting me, and as we sat there talking this guy who was in my block walked in to the visiting room to have a visit with his mom. This girl looked at me and said, "That's my uncle." "Small world," I thought. Her uncle and I became pretty good friends over time and he really looked out for me. But instead of being myself, I had to put on a show, and this show that I was about to put on resulted in one of those times I probably should have been killed.

One day this friend of mine asked me how much money I had stashed away stealing cars. He knew from his niece that I was convicted of a lot of stuff, but she failed to tell him that I was more of an idiot than a professional car thief. Instead of telling him the truth, I lied to him and told him that I was rich. Over about a month period, we talked about opening up a workout gym when we got out with the money I had, and he would run it. We even mapped out everything and got numbers of how much something like this would cost. Then one day he told his niece what we were doing and how excited he was that maybe he could finally get his life straight. His niece told him, "Scott is a liar. He doesn't have any money. His family will not even talk to him because he ripped them off to." When he came back from that visit he was extremely mad. I think the only thing that saved me from not getting killed or at least badly beaten was that one of his friends talked him out of it because he was going home pretty soon and I wasn't worth getting in trouble over. Also, I ended up going to another prison about a week after that. I guess I could say I was lucky.

SEVEN

MURDER FROM THE TOP

Shortly after that incident in the shower, I had a gang approach me and ask me if I wanted to become a part of them. I had always wanted to feel like I belonged to something and especially something as powerful as a prison gang, so I started the process of becoming one of them. But before that process took full effect, I ended up going to another prison. The prison I was transferred to was a known dump. There are certain prisons that guys don't want to end up in and this was one of them. Once I got to the prison someone saw the gang tattoo I had gotten at the other prison, and they took me in. I was now a fully fledged gang member. I became the property of one of the most violent prison gangs this country has to offer. Due to the oath I took to never leave this gang I will not refer to them by their name. I left on good terms, but some people wouldn't look at it that way, and besides I am not looking to glorify them. They do a pretty good job of that all on their own.

Being a gang member inside prison was like taking the good with the bad. If you were a part of an organization as I was, you never had to worry about someone messing with you. And if they did try, you had a whole lot of people backing you up. But with the good there is always the bad, and that bad was having to go on missions. Missions or hits were done by people like me. The guys who were the soldiers were the bottom of the totem pole. If someone needed to be stabbed or beaten they would call on us and we had to go do it. I say had to because that is exactly what I mean. There was no "I don't feel like it" or "I am going home next year so I don't want to get into trouble." If you didn't do what they told you to do, then you got dealt with. Sometimes that could be a beat down or them trying to kill you. Either way it wasn't pleasant.

One of these hits almost changed my life, and not for the good. This particular hit went really wrong and the guy who was in charge of carrying it out went after the wrong guy by mistake, and all Hell broke loose. Inside prison we had places to work out, and this particular prison had free weights. The guy who they were going after was not the guy working out on the bench that day, and this poor guy took a 50 pound weight right to his face. This guy was one of the leaders of the black gangs and as you can imagine, this wasn't going to turn out good for anyone. The next thing I knew both gangs were on the football field with knives in their hands ready to have a gang war. It got so out of control that the State police had to be called in, and they had their weapons drawn at us from the other side of the fence.

Allow me to add a side note here. An ex-corrections officer who was working that day at the prison when all this went down actually got a hold of me a few years back and asked me to speak to a group she put together of families who had loved ones coming home from prison soon. She told this story before I went on, and it was kind of weird working with her side by side because back then, she probably would have shot me if we hadn't complied with their orders.

I became real good friends with one of the guys in my gang, and he was pretty much as crazy as I was. We had this "I don't give a crap" attitude, and that's not a good attitude to have while serving time in a prison like we were in. When you get to a specific prison, you can't trust anyone, even the people in your gang. So when you do find someone you can trust, you do everything you can to make sure you don't screw that friendship up, because you never know when you might need them.

One day while we were walking the yard, we got word that one of the leaders of our gang was going to make us do a hit on a certain gang leader. For some reason the guy who controlled us at this particular prison hated me and my friend, so he was going to make us do this just because he could. Doing something like this is like going after a mob boss in New York. There was no way in the world that any good could come from this. Most major gangs had many members inside every prison in the state so even if we did this and they put us in another prison, it would be just a matter of time before we got killed. That day my friend and I walked the yard together and talked about this. Was there a way out? If we don't do it what would happen to us? If we did it and got caught how much time would we get for attempted murder or even murder? This was some real serious stuff and we needed to figure it out quickly.

We did find out that they were going to order us to do this hit on a Saturday. Weekends were always better to do things like this because there were only correctional officers working. There were no office people, no warden, no gang inspectors, and so on. We had 4 days until this was to go down, so we came up with a plan. But before that plan could go into effect we needed to get high. I guess pulling off a plan like this needed some type of stimulant, because no one in

56

their right mind would have even thought about doing what we were about to do.

As we sat around smoking a joint we discussed how this was going to go down. First we were going to tell the guy giving us the order that we would do it, knowing full well we had no intension of doing it. Secondly, we were going to get as much stuff on credit as we could from different people. What I mean by this is that inside of prison is kind of like a world of its own. Now I'm not too sure how prison is run today, but back in the early 90's we could get whatever we wanted. They had prison stores that we could buy stuff from – food, cosmetics, TV's, radio, tape players, clothes and so on. Instead of having cash we had tokens. Each token had different values from 25 cents to $20. You obtained money by working, or your family and friends could put money in your account by sending money orders or coming to the prison and depositing money into your account. Once a week we would fill out a form declaring how much money we wanted out of our account (up to $75), and we would get the tokens. If during the week you ran out of money you could go to what we called "store men." A store guy (and there were a lot of them) would loan you either tokens or food for a fee. The fee was 50 cents for every dollar you borrowed. We called it one and a half. It was expensive, but if you needed something you had no choice.

My friend and I had a lot of credit with these people because we were gang members, so we decided to get as much stuff as we could on credit before we put our plan into action. We went to every person we could get credit from and raked up a bill that was in the hundreds, not including all the pot we got on credit also. Once we did all that, we decided that we

57

needed to get off the prison yard; and the only way to do that was to put a story together that sounded so real that the prison officials would have no choice but to move us to another prison.

Prisons across the country have different levels of security. The either go by numbers or they call them minimum, medium or maximum. Michigan went by numbers 1-6. Level 6 was considered super max. There was only one prison considered level 6 in Michigan. Level 5 was maximum security, and the lower the number the lower the security. Most prisons also have what is called protective custody. Protective custody has its own classification and it basically makes sure that you never interact with the general population. Protective custody is used for a lot of reasons. Child molesters a lot of times end up there because the general population tries to kill them. Cops, judges and lawyers who go to prison go to protective custody for obvious reasons. And then there are guys like me and my friend. When you have a certain gang or multiple gangs looking to get a hold of you, the prison system doesn't mess around and they will put you in protective custody even if you don't want it. This is what was about to happen to us and we didn't even know it. The day before we were supposed to do this hit we had our plan in place and we put it in action. We both went to the correctional officers and told them our lives were in danger and we were about to get killed. That's all it took. They took us and put us in special cells where we were locked up 24 hours a day until the following Monday. Before anything else could be done we needed to wait for the gang inspector to come back to work, and that wasn't until Monday morning.

The inspector's jobs were strictly to follow gang activity throughout the prison; and they were the ones who decided if a person gets transferred to another prison or if they put you back to the same place you just left. I have actually seen guys get locked up in protective custody and instead of putting that guy in another prison, they transfer out the guy or guys who were trying to harm them. But the problem is that when you go to protective custody you must tell the inspector who it is that is trying to kill you. Telling on someone in prison is a death sentence of its own. You just don't do that.

Come Monday morning my friend and I were going to need to tell on someone, and that would pretty much put a price (hit) on us. No matter where we went we would be in danger. We knew this though, and we already had that figured out. Monday came around and here we were sitting in the inspector's office telling him what had taken place. We told the inspector that we had bought some pot from one of the dealers and we couldn't pay. When they asked us who the dealer was we told them that we didn't know because it was through one of the gangs and we only knew his street name. My friend and I knew they would buy this story because we were known gang members, and the last thing this prison wanted was another gang war. They had no choice but to transfer us to another prison. We didn't have to kill anyone and we didn't have to tell what really happened. And as far as the gang we were a part of, they had no idea what happened to us. They thought we got into trouble and so they simply sent us to another prison. As I look back at this I must say that even though I wasn't a believer and wouldn't be until many years later, I still see how God was working in my life. And I would continue to see His protection on me without even asking.

Eight
BACK TO REALITY

Being in prison and having to take orders from not only correctional officers but other inmates was just the daily routine we all had to go through. Prison was just one big routine. If that routine changed for whatever reason, we would get very agitated and it would throw us off completely. I remember one day as I was waiting in line to eat dinner that a guy in front of me must have had a problem with another gang, because someone came from in back of me and stuck a pencil right in this guy's jugular vein. You wouldn't think that a pencil could be used as a weapon, but when you stick it in the right place and it breaks off inside someone's neck it becomes very deadly. The fact that I just had just seen this and all that blood shooting out of this guy's neck didn't bother me. But what did bother me was the fact that the chow hall was now going to be closed and I had to wait to eat my dinner. There is a term that describes this type of mentality and it is called institutionalized. It means that you become so engrossed in your surroundings that the outside world and its values just don't matter anymore. The only thing that you care about now is what is going on inside prison. Once this happens to someone, it is very difficult to come out of prison and stay out.

Once a person is sentenced they have a certain amount of time that they must do. There are generally two numbers that are included in the sentence. The first number is the minimum time one must do before being eligible for parole. The second number is the maximum amount of years they can keep someone incarcerated. Going in front of the parole board once your minimum sentence is served is no guarantee that you will go home. The parole board looks at many factors in deciding if they are going to release you or retain you. The parole board has the option to give someone either a 12, 18 or 24 month continuance, meaning that you serve that amount of time past your minimum sentence.

The first time I went in front of the parole board they decided that I needed to spend another year in prison. They thought I wasn't rehabilitated enough. They told me I needed more programs like AA and NA. The parole process changed one year before I first met with them. Prior to this, it was fairly easy to get a parole. But now, because of the guy I talked about earlier that I was shackled to going to prison, Leslie Williams, it was almost impossible the first time around. Leslie Williams was released before his time and the parole board took the hit. When he got out he went on a killing spree which promoted an overhaul of the parole process. Leslie Williams some years later was stabbed over 17 times, and the word at the time was that it was because he screwed up the parole process. It is sad that no one cared that he raped and killed something like 13 girls. They just cared that they couldn't go home because of him.

The 12 additional months that I was given went by pretty quick. The incident at the prison where we had to stab that gang leader was taken care of. The guy that ordered us to do it was demoted to a lower rank because he had no right doing it. And I had to take a two minute violation for screwing up and not following the proper command. The two minute violation consisted of me getting beat everywhere but in my face. Trust me, if they could hit you in the jaw they would have, but that would be noticeable by the correction officers so they didn't. Violations were handed out quite a bit by gang leaders. That is how they controlled other members. If a member thought he had a chance of getting his ass whipped he was more careful about what he was doing and made sure he didn't screw up. I will be getting more into the gang life and how it operates in later chapters, but at this point in the story, I am finally coming home. The parole board decided it was time to send #226845 home. #226845 was my prison number and it is just like my social security number. It will be with me till the day I die. After I die they issue it to another inmate going into the prison system for the first time. Not a pleasant thought.

The day I was going home created probably the greatest feeling I have ever had in my life. I spent a lot of years being locked up and now in the matter of a few seconds (the time it takes to open the door) I would be free. Well almost free. I was on parole for two years, and I had to report to a parole officer once a month. But other than that I was free. Because I was three hours away from my mom's house I needed to take a bus home. My mom and stepdad decided to give me a chance to get my life right and that's where I was headed to. I remember the day like it was yesterday and I hope I never forget it. I hope I never forget that for one day I felt like a brand new person. I wasn't Scott the con artist/car thief. I was just Scott who had a new lease on life. It was a very amazing feeling.

I remember once I got to my mom's house that I needed to be alone. I needed to go and just hang out in a room and reflect on the day's events. I don't think anyone really understood that, but 12 hours earlier I had to look over my shoulder because at any moment I could have been killed; and now everyone just expected me to go back to normal. I didn't even know what normal meant. My mom asked me where I wanted to go eat and I picked out one of my favorite restaurants. I liked this place because it had a cafeteria type atmosphere. Kind of like what I just left. As we all sat down to eat I had some challenges right off the bat. For instance I hadn't eaten with real silverware for many years for obvious reasons, so the steel on my teeth kind of bothered me. The other challenge was all the people around me. In prison everyone is always looking out for the same thing you are, so they tend not to bump into you or reach over you to grab the salt. Here I had people bumping me, reaching over and around me and grabbing me and shaking my hand like it was everyday practice. I forgot how the "free world" acted. I needed a refresher course.

Another thing that really bothered me was shopping. I went to a mall with my mom a few days after being home and I couldn't take it, -too many people for me. It kind of goes back to the way it was at the restaurant. I basically just grabbed a bunch of clothes and got out of there. But as a few weeks went by I was back to the routine of life. I didn't know if that was a good thing or not. One thing I did know was that there was no way in the world that I had changed from who I was before I went to prison. Actually I was probably worse. I now had a street education and that education couldn't be taught in any classroom. It could only be obtained from where I just left, and that presented itself as a major challenge in everything I wanted to do or could do.

My parole officer was nothing like what I had heard about in prison. I always heard that these people played no games and they would lock your ass up if you sneezed wrong. When the parole officer came to my mom's house to check it out before I came home from prison she asked my mom, "What the hell is the matter with your son?" My mom has a very nice house and I didn't fit the bill of the average parolee. She was a very nice lady and she actually cared about me and her other clients. In prison you are just a number so I thought I would be a number out here also but I wasn't. When I first saw her she laid down the rules of parole and they were all pretty self explanatory. No weapons, no drug use, no drinking, must maintain employment and so on. I wasn't allowed to attend any place that served alcohol for obvious reasons, but she did say it was okay if I went to a restaurant that served alcohol. She didn't want me in bars basically. She told me, "If you do what you're told then these two years will go by quick. Don't lie to me and if you need my help just call." As I left that day I was pretty excited about my new future. I thought, "People really do care about me."

Nine

FALLING APART

My step-sister's boyfriend worked for a carpet cleaning company, and once I got home they lined a job up for me working with him. I actually liked working with him. He was a great guy and he never judged me about my past. I started to learn pretty quickly how to clean carpets, sofas, chairs and so on. Once I got the hang of this they sent me out on my own. I had a little machine that would fit in the back of my car, and I would take it in with me when I cleaned. Although the machine was small, it did a great job, and people were always impressed with the job I did. Every day I came home I felt like I finally had some worth. I worked hard at my job and it showed in my pay checks. I was making very good money and I opened up a checking account and get this it, was legal with my own name on it and everything. But I didn't want to clean carpets forever, so I decided I needed to get an education.

When I was a kid my mom was attending law school and the company she worked for dealt with medical claims and insurance. My mom took me to a few seminars that she had to attend for work. The seminars where held at a hospital and one of them had to do with cardiology. I sat through that seminar and I took notes. For some reason I actually understood what they were talking about and what I didn't understand I went home and looked up in an encyclopedia. I wanted to become a doctor after those seminars but I never pursued that avenue. I believe today that I was smart enough back then to become a doctor but I had no work ethic. And spending 8+ years in college didn't interest me to say the least. But that was back then and now I needed an education to get ahead in life. It was hard enough being an ex-con, but being an ex-con without an education was going to get me nowhere fast. So I decided to attend the community college by my house. I obtained my GED my second year in prison, and that's all I needed to attend the community college. Now all I had to do was pick a class. It didn't take me long to figure out the best class for me to start off with would be Criminal Justice 101. I thought I sure couldn't go wrong by taking this class. I could probably teach this class.

The class started on a Tuesday and I was extremely nervous because I haven't been in a school in years, let alone in a college. I had a problem though right from the beginning that no one else had. You are probably thinking my problem was not having been in a classroom for so long that I was at a disadvantage. That probably would have been the second problem, but we never got past the first.

The teacher opened up the text book and went through each chapter kind of giving a brief background of what that chapter was about and how it would all come together throughout the semester. First of all the easy class I thought I was taking was all about the other side of the criminal justice system. That's a side I never seen before. I was always in the back of the police car not in the front. Then the teacher got to chapter 13. I got real excited when I saw the title to this chapter-Community Correction. I smiled as I thought about the A+ I was going to get in this class. The teacher went into his lecture on chapter 13, but everything he was talking about was not even close to what I experienced for many years. I interrupted him and said something like, "Excuse me sir but I have to disagree with what you're saying here. I happened to know firsthand that's not how it really works." I forgot what he said to me but whatever it was it pushed a button, and I told him that he was a bitch and he could go screw himself and if he said one more word I would beat his ass. The problem I had right from the beginning was I still had my prison mentality, and if I didn't like what you said to me then I would deal with it by prison's rules not society's rules. Needless to say, I was kicked out of that class before it even began. After all this went down, if I had any self confidence it just went out the window. And it wouldn't be long after that I would be back to my old ways.

Rehabilitation is a b/s word the Department of Corrections tries to use when it comes to rehabilitating prisoners. There was no rehab that I knew of, and unless you consider AA or NA a rehab then that was about it. No one told me how to act once I came out of prison. I had to figure all that out on my own. I left some real good friends behind when I left prison and now since I was out on the streets, I had to find some new friends.

The first weekend I was home my sister invited me over to play cards with her and her friends. I loved to play poker when I was in prison so I was kind of excited to play out here with them. Everything was going great until the guy sitting next to me started talking about his job. He was a corrections officer in the women's prison. I didn't care what prison it was. He was still a correctional officer and I couldn't stand him. Everybody at the party laughed but me. I found nothing funny about sitting next to this guy, and he was lucky I didn't whip his ass. That night though I made some friends and the cool thing was no one judged me or made me feel like I was out of place. And till this day I often ask my sister how so and so is doing.

One Friday night I got a phone call from someone I met there and he wanted to know if I wanted to go to a bar with him and hang out. I knew I wasn't supposed to go to a bar but this place served food so I thought why not. I needed friendship and I was tired of hanging out by myself. We started hanging out quite a bit, usually on Fridays and Saturday nights, and we would go to different bars throughout the area. He was always asking questions about prison; and it seemed like I was always dodging the questions because I wanted to have a good time and forget about that life, but honestly aside from his questions, we had nothing really in common to talk about. One Saturday night we went to a hotel where a friend of his was having a party, and when we got there I kind of had to stand around outside because he was busy with one of his girlfriends. This girl's cousin also had to wait outside so we introduced ourselves and kind of laughed about the whole situation. We ended up talking that night and many more nights to come.

The company I worked for (cleaning carpets) was a sub contactor for a major retailer. Every morning we would go into the office and get our route for the day. We had to call all the customers for that day and let them know what time we thought we would be there. This was challenging because I worked all over the place and I still really didn't have a grasp of how long it took to do a certain job. I made sure though that if I was going to be late I would stop and call people to tell them. You would think they would have been mad that I was late but everyone was grateful that I called to tell them. This is a life lesson I still keep with me today.

One morning as I looked at my list of places to go, I noticed I had two pretty big jobs. I was kind of excited because this meant the boss was starting to trust me. I left that office feeling pretty proud of myself. As I sat in my car waiting for it to warm up I thought to myself, "Besides school, things are going good. I have a great job, I met a great girl and I have friends who actually like me." Life was pretty awesome or so I thought.

When I finished my morning job, the customer asked if they could use a credit card to pay the $400 bill. Most of my jobs were paid by credit card so it was no big deal. I would call the credit card number in and my boss would run it and that would be the end of that. I handed my customer a receipt and went to my second job. The second job I had was almost identical to the morning one. It was also a $400 job but they paid in cash so I didn't need to call it in. At the end of every day I would make sure all my paperwork was in order and I would turn it in. This particular day had trouble written all over it for me. I had $400 cash in my hand and no one knew about it but me and the customer. It was like a drug to me I needed that money. I hadn't committed a crime of any sort since being out of prison, and I literally had everything going for me but I was about to blow that. Even to this day I can't fathom why I wanted or needed that money. It was $400. I could see if it was a couple of grand but not $400. The second I justified me doing it I knew I would get caught, but like so many times before I didn't care. It was time to be all about Scott. Nothing mattered anymore but me.

I started to think about how I could pull this off. Then it hit me like a ton of bricks. I always kept a record of the credit card receipts in this book I had. When I wrote the receipt out for the customer it had all their information, and I had a carbon copy of that for my records. I went through the book and picked out a credit card number from another job I did the previous week that was close in price. I called my boss and acted like I just finished this job and told him the name and number on the credit card and how much the job was for. He never thought anything of it. He had a lot of guys working for him and he sure isn't going to remember a bunch of numbers and names from last week. I picked a job similar in price to pull this off because it would then look like someone screwed up and just double billed them. It is crazy how in the matter of seconds, I was back in the swing of stealing and conning people.

Between my regular job and stealing I started to make a lot of money, by my standards anyway. With that money I started to party and have a good time. The girl I was dating wasn't 21 yet so I had to party with my friends if I wanted to go to the bar. I started smoking pot once again and that was a violation of my parole, but I just didn't care. I also started doing pills. I would buy over the counter cold and flu medication and pop three or four of those a day. I liked the way they made me feel, and besides it wasn't a violation of my parole by taking cold medicine. I needed to cope with who I was becoming again, and any kind of drug or alcohol that would make me forget that was fine by me. I started to hang around my girlfriend more and more and the friends that I had kind of went by the way side. I am not a multi-tasker by any stretch of the imagination. It was impossible for me to have a girlfriend and friends at the same time, so I ditched the friends. It really wasn't hard though because I always just lived for the moment of what made me feel good, and being around her made me feel good.

I eventually got fired from my carpet cleaning job, - not for stealing, but for never showing up. I was still living at my mom's house at this time and I lied to her and told her I had been laid off. I also told her I had found another job but of course that was a lie. One day after hanging out with my girlfriend, I decided to go home. It was about 3:00 PM, and I knew my mom wouldn't be home until 5:00 PM. So I could go home and act like I just got off work.

As I pulled onto my street I noticed a few cop cars at the end of the block. I really didn't think anything of it because I hadn't done anything wrong in the city. So I dismissed it and pulled in front of the house. The second I turned the car off I had cops running at me from all directions. They pulled me out of the car as they had done so many times before and put their guns to my forehead. "If you freaking move I will kill you," one cop said. Another cop got on his radio and said, "We got him." "Got who?" I thought. "What did I do?" Once they got me handcuffed and threw me in the back of a police car, one of the robbery/homicide detectives came over to talk to me. He told me that a bunch of houses in the surrounding neighborhoods had gotten broken into and that morning the police dog tracked the scent of the robber between my mom's house and her neighbor. "One of the cops that were there this morning knows you and knows you just got out of prison." "Guilty by my past," I thought.

I told the cop, "This is B.S. I never broke into anyone's homes." But of course just because I said I wasn't guilty

71

didn't mean I wasn't. Every seasoned convict knows the first rule when getting arrested is don't say anything. Don't ever admit guilt. As I sat in back of that police car I saw a car approaching on the other side of the street and pull into my mom's driveway. It was my mom. She had gotten off work early and she came home to see all these cops at her house and me in the back of the police car. The police told her why they were arresting me and needless to say she was pissed. One of the police officers came back to the car and told me to swing my legs around and let them hang off the seat. He then proceeded to take off my shoe. I'm thinking what the heck does my shoe have to do with all this? The officer looked to see what the size was and then took it over to the detective. I couldn't hear what was said but the detective just shook his head and came back over to where I was. He told me to get out of the car and turn facing the police car. He took out a set of keys and unlocked my handcuffs and took them off.

At this point I had no idea what I what was going on. A few minutes ago they wanted to shoot me and now this. The detective explained that the reason why they were letting me go was because the person who was breaking into all the houses had a size 13 shoe and my size was a 9. He also explained why they thought it could have been me. My past record in the city, and me just getting out of prison, and the dog tracking right through our yard had me doing these crimes written all over it. I guess he had a point. Prior to going to prison I was arrested or detained by this city too many times to count. I made their most wanted posted in 1992, and they actually had a police officer who pretty much tried to follow me around all day long. One Saturday morning the SWAT team raided a hotel that I was staying in just to get me on some outstanding warrants I had. If you were to ask any police officer back then who they hated the most out of 100,000 people in the city, they would say without a doubt, Scott Mason. The detective told me to have a nice day. He never even apologized.

This incident was the last straw for my mom. She knew I was lying about my job and now this. She told me I had to leave by that night. I packed all my stuff up into my car and headed down the street. Of course I had nowhere to go, but unlike the past I had a car to sleep in. Good thing too, because it was cold and snowy that night. The next few nights I slept in various parking lots and rest areas along the highways. One particular night my girlfriend's mom and dad found out I was sleeping in my car and they told me I could stay with them until I got back on my feet. I was so excited because the night before it got down to something like 5 degrees and it was just too cold. My girlfriend's parents were laid back and they never judged me for being an ex-con. In their minds we all make mistakes and sometimes we all need a helping hand. In my mom's neighborhood which was considered upper class, you would be hard pressed to find someone to take you in or not judge you for your past. Here in my girlfriend's neighborhood, which was a mixture of lower and middle class people, they would help out in a second.

I guess that's just the way it is in America. Now I'm not saying that every person is like this in either area, but generally it goes down like that. As the cold months rolled into spring we found out that my girlfriend was pregnant. That didn't go over too well for obvious reasons. She was too young and I was just a piece of crap. But once everyone got over the initial shock it became an exciting time. You must remember I had no idea how to take care of myself, and now all of a sudden I have a child on the way. It was time to play house regardless if I was ready or not; and play house is exactly what we did.

We found out about a hotel not too far from her mom's house that rented efficiency rooms by the week. So we decided to move into one of them. The hotel wasn't too bad and it was in a decent neighborhood. One of the buildings had nothing but these efficiency rooms so everyone around us was either from out of town and temporarily working in the city, or they were in the same position that we were in.

I also found a job working at a gym down the street from where we were staying. I worked mostly days, and it allowed me to be home at night with her. Even though the place was nice I didn't trust anybody. After a few weeks we pretty much got settled in. We had an older couple who was from Texas next to us. They traveled state to state putting in fiber optic cable. They kind of took us in as family. I think because they didn't get to see their own kids too often they adopted us. I can honestly say I have never found a couple in my life that I grew attached to as I did them, and I often still think about them all these years later. He and I also had something in common, and that was smoking pot. He loved to get high and he always had some of the best pot around. We would get high every single night once we both got off work. My girlfriend didn't like it but she dealt with it. It mellowed me out. It was like my version of Ritalin.

One day he came over and told me he was getting a pretty big shipment in and asked me if I wanted to buy some to sell. Since he would get it from Texas, he tried to buy a few pounds at a time so he wouldn't have to keep on going back and forth.

I bought a few ounces and started selling pot. Selling and smoking pot was a definite one way ticket back to prison, and my parole officer by this time was pretty much sick of me screwing up and having dirty urines. Every time I went in to the parole office I had to pee in a bottle, and they would use a stick that would turn certain colors depending on the drug or drugs in your system. I had three dirty urine samples in a row, and I think that was the breaking point with her. She had given me enough leeway already, and the day I was supposed to report to her I called her and asked her if it was okay if I reported the next day because I had to work. Generally parole officers were pretty cool about meeting anytime that week because they understood that hours change or people work overtime. She told me, "No it isn't okay," and she said, "As a matter of fact, Scott, if you come in here my supervisor is going to arrest you and send you back to prison so don't ever come back."

I was very appreciative that she was honest with me and she probably had never done that before. But she liked me and knew I was about to have a child. I asked her what the next step was. She told me that after today there would be a warrant out for my arrest by the Corrections Division, and if I ever got pulled over and they ran my name, I would be arrested immediately and sent back to prison. She told me good luck. "You are a very bright young man," she said. "I hope you get it right some day." I never did tell my girlfriend about this, but from then on I had to be careful never to get questioned or pulled over by the police.

TEN

AND THEN THERE WAS 3

One morning my girlfriend woke me up and said that it was time. She was in labor. I was about to be a dad for the first time. We went to the hospital, and as a first time dad I really didn't know what to expect. But I did know that my life would be changed forever once that baby came into this world. Not too long after we checked in my girlfriend delivered. We had a beautiful healthy baby girl. I was so excited, probably a little too excited, because I went down to my car and smoked a joint. There was a reality that set in though when I was sitting in my car. We only had this hotel room we were living in and we needed an actual place like an apartment to raise a child, not some hotel room. But in the meantime this would have to do. Besides we had no choice. It wasn't like I had any money to do anything different. We went back home a few days later and a few things started to get interesting.

The gym I was working at had two buildings. Each building served a different purpose, and the one building that had all the gym equipment was the one I worked at. I was trusted enough to open and close the gym, so I pretty much got to do what I wanted without too much supervision. My boss was an ex-body builder who was about as cool as they came. He was a good looking guy who had tons of money, and his apartment and cars reflected that. He had a real bad ass Corvette that he would let me drive sometimes. One of the people that had a membership at the gym was a famous NHL hockey player. He would work out every single day and he and I became friends. At first I was pretty star-struck but after awhile I figured out that he was just a regular guy who had a real cool job. I'm not sure why he liked me so much. He was a multi-millionaire who signed autographs everywhere he went, and I was just a gym employee barely getting by. I think he liked me because I wasn't trying to get anything out of him or trying to use him in some sort of way. We were just friends who had nothing in common except the gym he worked out in.

One day after his work out he asked me if I wanted to go to this real nice bar down the street to have dinner. He was dating the bar tender there and he told her that he would stop in to eat. I was pretty excited to hang out with this guy. Up to this point it's only been in the gym. That night at this bar he treated me like one of his hockey buddies. He told me to order whatever I wanted and every time someone came up to get an autograph from him he would pass the item on to me to sign it. He told the people I was a rookie in the National Hockey League. For a few hours I felt like a real winner even though I really didn't play hockey. Some poor dude has on his wall my autograph and probably doesn't even have a clue that it's worthless. My friend liked to show off his money, and when we were finished with dinner he pulled out a stack of hundred dollars bills wrapped in a rubber band. He probably always kept thousands of dollars on him at all times. They were starting up the karaoke machine and he told me that for every song that I went up there and sang he would give me $100. But he got to pick the songs. I hated singing and could not sing, but for that kind of money I was willing to look like an idiot. I made out pretty good that night. He wasn't trying to make a fool out of me. He knew I needed the money and this was his way of helping me. I will never forget him and if he is reading this book I say, "Thank you brother. You were a true friend."

My girlfriend's grandma decided we needed an apartment and she helped us get into one. She helped us by signing the lease and paying the deposits to get in. It was actually nice to be in a place that we could call home, but I truly missed the friends I made at the hotel. One of the stipulations of her grandma helping was I had to get a job. As you look back on everything that you have read so far you get the idea and I've said it, that lying was almost like a game to me. I would go to great lengths to cover up a lie.

This next lie that I told could possibly be the craziest one I have ever told and the craziest one I ever tried to pull off. I told everyone, including my girlfriend, that I was hired by Ford Motor Co. I would be working the assembly line on the day shift. Now there are a few different reasons as to why I told such a crazy lie. I was sick and tired of people looking at me as being worthless as I had proven time and time again, and I figured if I had a job like this everyone would look at me as a provider for my family. Again I only lived for the moment. The day that I supposedly started this job I needed to go down to the local flea market and get one of those long blue jackets that Ford employees wore. I found one that was similar but I needed a name plate and Ford logo plate. I found what I was looking for and I headed to the store for a needle and some thread. I sat in a parking lot and I stitched the patches right on to the coat. It actually looked like I worked at Ford Motor Co. During the days I would sit in the parking lot of the Ford Motor plant that I was supposedly working for just in case someone came by to see if I really worked there. I did this same thing years ago when I was living at my dad's house. All this worked out pretty well up until it was time to get paid.

Again I have no idea why I went through all this time and time again. Trust me it wasn't because I was lazy, because I really had to work hard at pulling these scams or lies off. I used to think a lot about why I did what I did, but after awhile I just gave up. I had to tell everyone the truth about the job and how I lied. My girlfriend didn't have time to be too pissed off though because our rent was a few months behind and we were about to get booted. The date was right around the corner and we needed money.

Today you can go to almost any store and return an item that you don't have a receipt for and they will give you an in store credit, which means they will give you a store credit card that has the exact amount that your item was for and you can only spend it there. Back then they gave out cash. If you walked into a store and returned a pair of jeans that were $40 and you didn't have a receipt, they would give you the $40. Most major stores operated like this. The only thing was they would track your returns in their system by your driver's license or ID, and once you had 3 or more returns without a receipt they would turn you down. Back then though stores didn't have a computer system that linked the stores together so there was no way one store could know what the other store was doing. I literally set out to steal as much merchandise as I could and went to as many stores as I could. We needed over a thousand dollars within a week so I had no choice but to do this. I started off stealing the smallest items that cost the most. I would steal five or six of the same item from one store and return them to several different locations. I literally stole stuff every single day, and before I knew it I had made enough to pay the rent. I wish it would have stopped there, but what I found out while doing this was I was good at it. Once again it turned out to be a game, and even if I didn't need to steal something I still did. The stores though became aware of what I was doing, and one by one they stopped returning the items I would bring in.

It didn't take us long to get behind on our rent again, and without being able to steal from any more stores, we were in trouble. The apartment management would put notices in our mailbox about being evicted but I would just throw them out. My girlfriend had no idea but I knew, and my days were spent looking for the bailiff and the guys who did the evicting. One afternoon while she was at work and I was watching our daughter there was a knock on the door. It was the bailiff. They were there to put our stuff on the side walk. I had just got done watching them evict the guy a few doors down and they didn't walk anything down the stairs. It all went over the railing. I'll be honest; even as I write this I have tears in my eyes. How could I have allowed this to happen? My child's crib was going to be throwing off the railing and there was nothing I could do about it. The bailiff walked into the apartment and looked around. The next words out of his mouth shocked me and I think it shocked him too. He said, "You have a very nice apartment with a lot of nice things. If I put them on the sidewalk people will steal them. I will go talk to the landlord of this place and ask them to give you to the weekend to get out. Will you promise me you will be out by the weekend?" I said, "Yes sir I will". He said, "If I have to come back here and you're not out it's not going to be good for you." Once he left I sat down on our couch and cried. I had no problem messing up my life but now that it involved my girlfriend and child well that was just another story. A story that will bother me till the day I die. I owe a lot of people a debt of gratitude over the years but the bailiff I owe a big one because if he didn't do what he did I planned on killing myself that night.

Over the next few weeks I lived from hotel to hotel and my girlfriend moved back home with her mom and dad. I didn't get to see my daughter every day, and even though I put myself in this situation I still cared for her deeply. I was an addict. I was addicted not only to getting high whether that was drugs or alcohol, but I also was addicted to crime, to the suspense, to never knowing what was going to happen next. I was addicted to the lifestyle, and the lifestyle had just taken the only thing that really mattered to me, my daughter.

The car that I had was the one that my aunt gave me. It was almost on its last leg but it was a station wagon, and if I didn't have a place to sleep I slept in back of that. One day while coming back from trying to make some money the car broke down. I was able to push it into a business parking lot to try to fix it. It was dead. This was the only thing I had. It was my house, it was my closet, and it was my dining room. It kept me safe and out of the elements. Most of all though, it allowed me to see my daughter. Without that car I was screwed. Seriously when I say screwed, I mean beyond screwed. I had no one to help me. I couldn't call somebody to help me. I had burned every bridge possible.

I sat there for awhile trying to figure out what I was going to do. There was a car dealership about a block down from where I was and that was my ticket. I grabbed a nice shirt from the back of my car and walked into the dealership. I picked out the guy I thought I could get over on and gave him the talk I thought about as I walked there. I told him I was looking for a black escort (one I already seen on the lot) and I told him I was paying in cash. When you tell a salesman you are paying in cash they get excited. He pulled the car around that I had seen in the parking lot and handed me the keys. "Go ahead and drive it for a few miles and see if you like it," he said. I took the car and went right across the street to my old car and loaded it up with all my stuff. Just before I left I looked at my old car which represented my old life. I reminisced about my daughter and my family. Because the minute I drove off in the car I was test driving, it would be one of the last times I would see my daughter for many years. I already had a warrant for my arrest from the Corrections Department, and now I was about to add that by stealing this car. I had no choice; I swear I didn't. I got out of the city as fast as I could before the cops could come looking for me. It wouldn't take long for them to find me though.

I was staying at a hotel one night and across from the hotel was a bar/restaurant. I hadn't eaten in a while because I was out scamming and stealing and trying to get money to survive. So I decided to go over to this place and eat. It was already late and by the time I got there they were just about to shut the grill down. I ordered my food and had a few drinks. I was more into doing drugs than drinking, but I decided to have a few anyway. Because I hadn't eaten pretty much all day, the alcohol kind of hit me harder than usual, and I became a little drunk. "Not a big deal," I thought. "I am staying right across the street and it's not like I'm falling down hammered."

I got into my car, looked at the time (2:02 AM), and headed out of the driveway toward my hotel. Just as I was about to pull out a police officer drove past me. Now any other time I would have acted normal, but I had been drinking and I wasn't thinking straight. I put the car in reverse and went and parked in the back of the building. I figured I would give the cop a few minutes to drive down the street before I left. I smoked a cigarette and thought enough time had passed. But the minute I drove out on to the street heading for the hotel I saw lights in my mirror. I was getting pulled over. I wasn't 200 feet from my hotel door. I was so close that when I pulled over it was in front of my room.

The cop got out and told me why he was pulling me over. He said he saw me put the car in reverse and hide out in back of the building once I saw him. He said the only person that would do something like that was someone who had something to hide. "Man if he only knew," I thought. Here is the thing though. He never ran the cars plate or me through his criminal check. He just assumed I was drunk. He had no idea that I was a wanted man or in a stolen car. He put me through the standard walk the line and follow my finger test, and then he administered the breathalyzer test. I blew a 1.1. Back then drunk driving was 1.0, not a .08 like today so I really wasn't that drunk, but I was drunk enough to get arrested. He handcuffed me and put me in the back of the police car. I knew what would happen next. He now had my driver's license in his hands. He ran my name and what popped up kind of scared him because he wasn't expecting me to be this bad ass. I think after all this he was probably the most cautious cop in the world. He would pull over some old lady and handcuff her for speeding until he found out she was safe.

The officer did something that night that I have never seen before. After he found out all about me he turned around and started talking about why I was getting into so much trouble. He told me that I seemed like a real nice guy and if I wanted to have a future the sky was the limit. I have heard this so many times when I would get arrested. I wasn't the average ex-con and it perplexed people why I was in so much trouble all the time. The officer knew I was going back to prison and he told me, "I am going to do you a major favor. If I charge you with drunk driving you will not be able to drive when you eventually get out of prison, and it's going to be hard enough on you when you get out as it is." I said thank you.

And then I asked him for a favor. I told him "My room is right in front of us. Can you please allow me to go in there and call my girlfriend and tell her I am being arrested and going back to prison. I can't call collect to their house. They have a block on the phone. Please officer I have a child and she is going to worry about me." He thought about it for a second and got out of the car to let me out. "I can't take the handcuffs off Scott but I will dial for you and put the receiver to your ear. You better not try anything stupid." I said I wouldn't. He opened the door and identified himself as a cop and when he thought it was safe we proceeded in. He did exactly what he said he would do and I got to say good bye one last time. I told her to kiss our daughter and tell her that I really do love her. Just before we left I had some change and a few dollar bills on the dresser. I said, "Officer would you please pick that up and take it with us. It's all the money I have in the world." As he did he looked at me with sadness in his eyes.

84

Eleven

HERE I GO AGAIN

I was sentenced by the judge to 1 ½ to 5 years for the stolen car. This time around, because I had such a low sentence, I would be sent to one of the prisons way up in the Upper Peninsula of Michigan. This would be nothing like my first time in prison. The prisons up there were considered level 1 (minimum security) and they would allow inmates to work outside of the prison. After I did my five week stay in Jackson prison to get classified they sent me North. North meant a 12 hour ride on a Grey Hound bus, but Grey Hound didn't own it the MDOC did, and it had a few modifications. When an inmate was on that bus he was shackled as we would say from head to toe. Besides being handcuffed and leg shackled there was a black box they put over the handcuffs so you couldn't try to pick the lock. The black box had a chain that was connected to your waist so the only movement you had with your hands was a few inches at best. If you had to itch your nose you needed to bend your head down as far as it would go just to reach your fingers. The leg shackles were like handcuffs for your legs. It had a very short chain that went between each leg and that was just in case you tried to run you would trip over yourself. Just to make sure that you wouldn't try to run they had one more security measure in place. From the leg shackles was another piece of chain that connected to the floor of the bus. Literally you became a part of the bus. If that bus flipped over at any time and started on fire you would be dead in a second. If you're wondering how we used the bathroom well let's just say that a syrup container that you might see at a restaurant became our best friend. The worst part of this 12 hour trip was it was 12 hours from point A to point B. The bus never went from point A to point B. There were about 30 other prisons in between where I was headed and they stopped at every single one to either pick up or drop off inmates. The 12 hour ride turned into 20. Till this day I will never ride on any type of bus for a long distance. I would rather walk.

The prison that I was at was located near Copper Harbor, which is the Northern most part of Michigan. If you look at a map of the state of Michigan and you see the tip, that's basically where I was. Most people don't know this but Michigan has two different times zones, Eastern and Central. I was in Eastern but not too far away was a town called Crystal Falls and that's where the Central time zone started. The winters up there were brutal. I actually went to bed one night at about 10:00 PM with no snow on the ground and woke up at 6:30 AM to see 26 inches of snow on the ground. Besides being cold, the wind chill because of the lakes was always below zero. This specific prison was more of a working camp than a prison. It was an honor to be in a place like this, and one minor infraction would get you kicked out and put into an actual prison. There was one fence that surrounded the prison itself, but it was more for show than anything. There was only one escape in all the years that the prison was open; and the man that escaped came back 3 hours later because it was too cold and he had no idea where he was going. To say this place was in the middle of nowhere is an understatement. It just sucked, but it beat being locked up in a cell all day long. I had to learn a few things in this prison and the number one thing I learned was a work ethic. If I wanted to stay here I would have to throw everything out the window I thought I knew about working. It was time to become a man.

I signed up for the logging position they had open at the prison. I didn't know anything about cutting down trees but it sounded like it would be interesting, so I asked if I could become part of the team. The man that ran this specific job was a logger for 25 years before becoming a Correctional Officer, and he looked like it. He even had an attitude that went with that look. I have met some real jackass people in my life but this guy took the cake. Seriously if you looked up jackass in the dictionary there would be a picture of him next to the word. But as I soon learned he needed to be that way, because people's lives were on the line every second of every day out in the woods.

Once I met with him he asked me some basic survival questions. He wanted to see if I would be smart enough not get myself or others killed out there. He looked at me for a moment and said, "Okay you're hired. We start at 6:00 AM and you had better have dressed warmly." The prison supplied all the clothing we needed for a particular job and once I got what I needed I tried to put it on. My first morning didn't start out to well. As I said I tried to put the clothing on, but I couldn't figure out what the padded pants where so I asked. My boss just shook his head and walked away. Another inmate who I was working with told me that they are called chaps and they protect you from the chain saw taking off your leg. Imagine my surprise when I heard that. I never worked a chain saw before and here I'm thinking I might come back tonight minus a leg. "What did I get myself into?" I thought.

Over the next few months I learned what my job was all about. There was a crew of 6 of us that would go out into the woods and cut down trees for a major paper company. The company had a contract with the department of corrections and the 6 of us were that contract. We would start in one spot and completely clear out the trees and set them aside for the loggers to pick up. It wasn't as easy as it sounds though. When I first started I thought I would just go out there and cut a tree down. Man was I wrong. There is an actual science to all this and as I would l learn, gravity was my best friend. My first few months on the job consisted of picking up all the branches that were cut off the trees. It was a nonstop job. Each one of us had a job to do and became like a production line of sorts. One guy cut the trees down, 2 others would cut off the branches, and the rest of us would take the branches to the street to be chipped up in the chipper. Back and forth we did this for 10 hours a day. I learned a lot though, and as spring approached I was about to be taught a few valuable lessons that I would never have thought of growing up in a city.

One morning before we started work our boss had a few pointers for us. He went on to tell us since the thaw was coming we would be moving to a new area and this new area had a lot of bears roaming around. He also told us that some hadn't awakened from their hibernation yet, so some could be still in the trees that we were cutting down. I guess bears like to hibernate in the hollows of big trees that are dead already. He also told us what to do if we came across a bear or her cubs, "Drop and play dead. It's your only chance. If you run they will catch you," he said. I wish I could have videotaped my expression once I heard all this. The second pointer had to do with bees. He told us that as the spring turned into summer the bees would either have their hives in dead wood on the ground or in the trees. He said if we were to come across a hive and we disturbed it we needed to run as fast as we could and not to stop running until the bees stopped chasing. He said bees will generally only chase up to a certain point. "Great," I thought "This should be an interesting summer."

As the summer months approached and it got hotter, it became very hard to work. Most jobs you could dress as the season permitted, but our job didn't allow us to do that. We still had to wear all the protective gear that was required by law. My protective gear that summer had an added feature, a fall harness. A harness is a device that would wrap around your legs and body and it would connect to a stable object up to six feet and it stops you from falling to the ground. Getting the harness meant I was being promoted. I was now the one who would cut down the trees. No more busting my butt taking branches to the street. A couple of things happened once I was promoted. The boss who I said was a jackass now treated me with respect, and he sat me down and told me why I was getting this promotion. He almost talked to me like I was his son. He asked about my life and what got me sent to prison and then he said something I had never heard anyone tell me before. He said, "I believe in you. This is why you are getting this opportunity." No one had ever told me they believed in me. Those words were like gold to me. Every day that I didn't feel like going to work I just thought about what he said I would be up and dressed ready to go.

It's amazing how a few words of encouragement can really change someone's life and how they view themselves. My

89

time was coming to end though working in the forestry division of the department of corrections. It was time to go home. If you are working out in the free world like I was, the parole board didn't even request to sit down and interview you for a parole. They just gave you one. It was the only time I was ever sad about leaving a prison. I had made some good friends and even my boss who I disliked in the beginning became a friend. Just before I left the prison my boss came over to where I was standing and leaned into me and said once again, "Scott I believe in you. Now go out there and get 'em.'

Twelve

NEVER HAD A CHANCE

My dad was waiting for me at the bus station in downtown Detroit. This time I was on a real Grey Hound bus, and as we pulled up all I could think about was getting some real food. Funny how something as trivial as a hamburger from McDonalds can mean so much to someone who has been locked up for any amount of time. As I got off the bus my dad and I hugged and headed toward his house. I really don't remember why my dad decided to help me out this time. Maybe my mom called him and said someone had to help me, or maybe it was just because I was his son. Either way, I needed it; and I was appreciative that someone cared. My dad took me out to eat and there we talked about how he was going to help me. We really didn't have a plan so we figured we better start with a place to live. We did need to find a place for me to live that day because my dad's wife made it very clear that I wasn't allowed to stay at their house, not even for one night. We went through the phone book trying to find a hotel that charged by the week and had a kitchen in it. After a few hours of looking we came across a place a few miles away from where he lived.

To be honest though, I was at a disadvantage right from the beginning. In order to get out of prison you have to give the parole board an address where you are going to live. They will never release you to the streets, so my dad allowed me to put his address down knowing full well I wouldn't be staying there. The second problem, besides lying to the parole board and my parole officer, was the hotel that we chose for me to live in. My dad asked my parole officer before I came home, "If Scott finds his own place to live can he move out of my house." My parole officer said that was fine, but he gave my dad a rundown of places I was not allowed to live, and the number one place on that list was the place I was going to. I'm not home 12 hours and I had already broken enough rules to get me sent back to prison that day. But we had no choice so I moved into my new home.

I saw rather quickly why my parole officer said no to this place. My neighbors where hookers, drug addicts and drug dealers. There were a few times that I had to walk over people that where passed out in the hall ways; but just like I had in prison, I would mind my own business. I knew that this wasn't going to last, but I didn't have time to think about that. I needed to get ready to go meet the man who would control my life for awhile.

My parole officer came straight out of hell. Seriously, when people would ask me who my parole officer was they would make a crazy face and then say, "Sorry man." This guy had a record of sending more people back to prison then any parole officer in the state of Michigan. He was like a drill instructor, and he even looked like one. I am shocked to this day that he is even still alive. I figured some crazy parolee would have shot him by now.

The thing with this guy and why people hated him was because he gave no leeway. It wasn't like he went out of his way to send you back to prison, but the minute you screwed up he handed your ass to you on a silver-plate. I thought to myself, "If I can just do what he says, I will be alright." My first visit to him also included my dad. He wanted to make sure that my dad and I were very clear on his rules. I think my dad couldn't figure out if he should shake his hand or salute him when we sat down. The parole officer went on a 10 minute rant about how I should be locked up for life because of all my felony convictions but there was nothing he could do about that. He also made it clear that he would do everything in his power to make sure I got sent back to prison. He said I was his worse case yet and he will not sleep till I was back behind bars. 24 hours earlier I have a correctional officer telling me how much he believed in me, and now I have a parole officer basically telling me I am a piece of crap. "Oh well", I thought, "I only have to see this guy once a month so I can deal with it."

I think his speech to my dad and I was more of a put on than anything. I think he wanted to scare me enough to stay out of trouble. Once he went through all the rules about getting a job and not hanging out in bars, he asked us if we had any questions. "No sir", I said. He got up from the chair and put himself right in front of me as if to size me up. He put his hand out and I shook it, and he said, "Good luck." From there we went back to the hotel that would have got me sent back to prison if he would have known about it.

Since I didn't have a car I needed to get a job within walking distance of where I was living. I applied at two grocery stores and I figured at least one would hire me. Well within a two day period both places wanted to hire me, so I took both jobs. One job was working midnights stocking shelves, and the other was afternoons also stocking shelves. It worked out pretty good as far as scheduling went. There were only a few times that I had to go from one job to the other. I figured this would most definitely keep me out of trouble. On top of all this, my parole officer made me attend some drug counseling crap which was on the other side of town. This was a mandatory four month class that met once a week. The two hour class turned into about five hours for me by the time I took all the different buses to get there. I hated this class but I had no choice.

One day while I was seeing my parole officer he told me that he had my progress report from the drug class. Once a month the teacher would send him a report on how I was doing. The report said nothing but good things about me. This report kind of got my parole officer off my back slightly. He was impressed that I was working two jobs and attending this class but as I said, only slightly. He still reminded me that I would probably screw up and return to prison. This guy should have been in the Army as a drill instructor not a parole officer. I left that day with a little smile on my face. I figured if I could impress him just a little I must be doing something right. As I walked out of that office I noticed the trees and flowers across the street at the court house. It was fall and the leaves were changing colors. I had been so busy that I hadn't even noticed that it was getting close to winter.

Thirteen

LIVING ON BORROWED TIME

A guy that I worked with at one of the grocery stores asked me if I wanted to go to a bar he knew of. It was on the water and they served food, "So it's not like you'll get into trouble," he said. But unlike my first parole officer who allowed me into places that served alcohol and food, this parole officer wasn't buying into that. He told me from the beginning that he didn't even want me in a store that served liquor. Obviously he couldn't enforce that because both places I worked at served liquor, but he got his point across. But honestly I didn't see a problem with going to this bar and besides I had been either working or cooped up in the hotel room and I need some fun in my life.

The bar that we went to that night was actually pretty cool. It was right on the water and I basically grew up around water, so as I looked across the lake I reminisced about the good times I had growing up. I loved to water ski and I wondered if I would ever have the chance to do it again. Just then I caught a glimpse of a girl across the bar looking at me. Now I am not shy by any stretch of the imagination but it had been some 21 months since I had any real interaction with someone of the opposite sex. I told my friend that I was going to over there to talk to her. Just before I was about to do so, the waitress came over and handed me a drink. I told her I didn't order it and she said it was from the girl over there, the one who I was going to go talk to. Before I went, my friend reminded me that I better have a better story than just getting out of prison. I agreed. How could I bend the truth without really lying?

I went over to where she was standing and introduced myself. It was pretty loud where we were standing, but the place was packed and we had nowhere else to go. It worked out good though. With it being so loud it left the conversation to a minimum. Before I knew it was 2:00 AM and the bar was closing. I was having such a good time just hanging out there that I didn't want it to end. As we were saying our good byes, she told me that her friend owned a house on the lake and they were all going back to his house to party a little. She asked me if I wanted to go. This had problems written all over it.

First of all this girl was a lot older than me, and she was already established and successful in life. And her friends were the same way. All I had to offer someone was how not to get raped or stabbed in prison. The second thing was, I didn't have a car. I did have a driver's license but no car, and as far as I could see it would be a while before I could get one. I told her that sure I'll go, but my friend had driven me there and she would need at some point to give me a ride back home. And then I thought for a second. Home. Home was a hooker infested hotel. "Oh well," I thought, "I will figure that out later." She agreed and off we went.

Once we got to the house I didn't feel like being around a lot of people, so I asked her if she wanted to sit on the deck overlooking the lake. We sat there the whole night just talking about life; well, her life. My life was one lie after another. Every time I opened up my mouth another lie came out and pretty soon I didn't even know who I was. She asked what I did for a living and instead of being honest, I told her I worked

96

as an undercover cop. She asked me where I lived and I told her a subdivision name that was by the hotel I stayed in. She asked me what kind of car I had and I told her I drove a motorcycle. I figured if I said a motorcycle she would never ask me to pick her up. I tried to cover all my bases with her, and it seemed to work. The problem with all this was she really seemed to like me and I either would continue down this b/s path or just get rid of her.

After that night we started to see each other quite a bit. We would either go out to eat or maybe hang out at a bar, but we never went back to her place and we surely never went back to mine. I could just see her coming over there. "Don't mind the passed out hooker, just step over her." That wouldn't go over too well. Besides I started to like her and I didn't want to screw this up. Kind of late for that I know, but I had no other choice. I probably should have just gotten with one of the hookers in my building. I wouldn't have had to lie to them.

Besides dating someone who I have been lying to from the beginning things were still going good. I was working a lot of hours at my two jobs, and I made my weekly drug meetings. But in order to spend more time with the girl I was with, I needed to think of something. I decided I would work less hours at my afternoon job so that way we could at least have dinner together. She had no idea what my hours were since she thought I was an undercover cop so I would just tell her I made my own hours. I knew that at some point this was going to come to an end, but I was kind of slipping back into my old ways so I started to care less and less.

One night she invited me over to her house for dinner and as usual since she didn't know where I lived, I had her pick me up at the corner of the subdivision. I always told her until I got to know her better I didn't want her knowing where I lived since I worked undercover. She never questioned it. After dinner she asked me if I wanted to smoke a joint. Can you believe this? She was asking an undercover cop if he wanted to smoke a joint. Well she didn't know I wasn't a cop. I could of just said no or told her I get drug tested at work but I didn't. I smoked that joint with her. I knew that I had to go see my parole officer 2 days later but I was just living in the moment and not thinking ahead. Once I got home that night and the high went away I thought, "Oh man, I'm screwed." The drill instructor of a parole officer I had was right all along. He would eventually send me back to prison and it was just a matter of time.

Back when I was on parole the first time I remembered I beat a few urine tests by using a product that would coat my system for up to 90 minutes. This product wouldn't clean me out but it would act as a masking agent so when they would test my urine it would come up clean. The only problem I had was getting this stuff. I only knew of one place to get it and that was a little over an hour from where I lived and I only had 24 hours to get it. I needed a plan. I told my girlfriend that I needed to go get this stuff because my work called in a drug test. She felt so bad that she had gotten me high that she took off a half of day of work just to take me down there. In order for this product to work properly I need to take the four pills two hours before I was to take the test and I had to drink 16 ounces of this crap they called a drink one hour before. If done properly it would last up to 90 minutes. The problem with this stuff they had you drink was you couldn't throw it up and every single time I took a drink I felt like I had to throw up. It was that bad. I can't explain it but I wouldn't think that drinking motor oil would be too far off from this.

The other potential problem was what if I had to sit in the parole office for more than 90 minutes. I guess it was just the chance I had to take. That morning as I got ready I was so nervous that I had trouble brushing my teeth and once I got to the parole office you could probably here my teeth chattering. My parole officer called me into his office as he usually did and asked the basic questions. I kept wondering if he knew that I got high. "He's smart. He knows. I'm going back to prison. I know it." My mind was racing a million miles an hour, but I couldn't help it. Then we did what we did every month. We went back towards the bathroom to do my urine test. I would take the cup into the bathroom and he would stand outside the door watching to make sure I didn't put someone else's urine in the cup or mess with the cup in anyway. When I was done I walked over to the table where he would test it. Till this day I can remember everything about those few minutes. This would either go one of two ways. Number one, I would be eating dinner with my girlfriend that night or number two, I would be eating dinner with a bunch of guys in the county jail and I hated the county jail. I didn't mind prison but I hated that county jail. My parole officer pulled out the stick that would send me home or to jail and stuck it in the urine. Usually if the urine had drugs in it would take a little longer to change color to show that. The color I didn't want to see was blue and mine was showing up blue. But it had to sit in there for two minutes. In those two minutes he talked to me about the drug classes I was taking. He wanted to know if it was working. I thought, "Well in about 30 seconds you're going to know if they are working." He took the stick out and wrote on his paperwork the date, time and the result of the test. Negative. He told me to have a nice weekend and he would see me next month.

I wish I could say that I learned something from this. I beat the drug test and that was that but of course I had to push it to the max. So instead of learning I went out and got an ounce of pot. I smoked more pot in that weekend then I think I ever had in my life. I would worry about next month's urine test next month I thought. I started to slip back into my old ways rather quickly. Not just because I was getting high but my mental state was getting real close to saying, "Screw it". Because I was spending more and more time with my girlfriend, I quit my afternoon job all together and my night job wasn't going too good because if I was out partying with her on a Friday or Saturday night, I would call into work and tell them I was sick. I also started stealing cigarettes at my night job and I think they knew it but just couldn't prove it. One of the nights I actually did go to work they met me at the door. They fired me and told me I wasn't allowed in the store any more. They never did give a reason but I knew why. One of the guys I worked with was a friend of mine and he later told me that they just had enough of all the games I was playing.

"Hey no problem," I thought. I didn't like that job anyway, but the problem with that thinking was I had no way to pay my rent at the hotel and the second someone was late at this place they were out. I needed to figure something out before this happened to me. That night I received a phone call that solved my living arrangements. My girlfriend had to go out of town for work training for a few days and she asked me if I would house sit for her. She had two dogs and she didn't want to have to put them in a kennel while she was gone. I played it off like I really couldn't but in the end I told her I would. I didn't want her to think I was desperate. I packed up my clothes and the few belongings I did own and turned in my key to the hotel desk. I was doing one thing right I thought. I am not living in the place my parole officer said I couldn't live in a while back.

The couple night stay at my girlfriend's house turned into a regular thing. I wasn't living there but I was if that makes sense. I had planned this all along. I knew once I got in there she wouldn't kick me out but at the same time I didn't want to screw this up, so I got the newspaper one day and started looking for a room to rent in someone's house. I needed a place to go every so often and I needed a place to store my clothes and things. I found one pretty cheap in this ghetto community and I sort of moved. One day while we were having dinner I told her that I wasn't going to renew the lease on my house, the house that she never seen. And I told her I was going to rent a room in the hood so I could save money. I told her that my dream was to buy my own house someday and the only way to do that was to live cheaply for awhile. She agreed and was all on board with my decision. I knew that once she saw this room I had rented she wouldn't want me staying there and she would have me move in with her. I took her one Saturday afternoon to the place I had rented and sure enough she told me that she didn't want me living in that neighborhood. When we pulled up there were people on the porch next door drinking and selling crack. She wanted me to move in with her but instead of telling her yes, I said I would need to think about it.

This was my life; this is what I lived for. I played games with people's lives and emotions. I wasn't good at it, I was great at it. All this was like a chess match to me. I would always have two or three moves already worked out ahead of time and when I got what I wanted I would move on to the next adventure. I didn't care about anybody but myself. I would come rolling into someone's life like a tornado and when I was gone the devastation was unreal. My girlfriend who I have been talking about was an adventure and since I got what I ultimately set out to get it was time to move on. But I wasn't going to give up living with her. After all, I needed a place to stay. The move on part I am referring to was finding another woman to con. I needed an older woman who had some money. I had a place to live; now I needed cash. Where would I find a woman like this? I had to do some research and I had to do it quick. I had $7 left to my name.

My monthly parole meeting was coming up and I knew that I was going to get into trouble since I missed my last two meetings for my drug classes. I had a lot of reasons for not going but my parole officer wasn't going to buy any of them. One of the stipulations of my parole was to complete these classes or I would go back to prison and on top of that, I smoked way to much pot that month and I knew that I had to either get the product that helped me beat the test or just not report. If I didn't report when I was supposed to then I knew my parole officer would put out a warrant for my arrest that day. As I said before he did not give second chances. The other thing I knew would happen is I wouldn't be able to talk to my dad anymore. If I missed parole my parole officer would be calling him or going to his house to find out where I was since he thought I was still living there, and my dad then would find out I was back to my old ways. This was a no win situation. I knew one thing though. I was not about to volunteer to go back to prison and if I showed up that's what would happen.

My parole date came and I was nowhere to be found. As of that afternoon my parole officer put a warrant out for my arrest. I was used to having warrants out for me but this warrant was a little different. This warrant stated that I was wanted for absconding (meaning not showing up) and it also stated that I was a known gang member who should be considered armed and dangerous. The parole officer lied his butt off on this warrant because I never had any violent felonies in my past, and he was using my prison record against me which he shouldn't have done. What this warrant did was this. Instead of them arresting me if I got pulled over, they came looking for me. A priority warrant goes out to all police agencies in Michigan and my face was in every city across the state. They were coming for me.

Having this warrant out for my arrest changed my life completely. I had to watch myself at all times and my girlfriend started to notice. Not too long after this I think her sister and friends also started to question some things about me and once they started talking among themselves nothing added up. It was like a complex puzzle. If they looked at all the pieces individually it made no sense but once they started putting it together it showed the whole story. Day after day my girlfriend would question me about certain things and it just came to a point that I couldn't keep up with all the lies. One night after work she told me that she needed some time apart from me. She asked me to find someplace else to stay while she thought all this through, and she said she would contact me when she was ready. This totally threw me off guard and I wasn't too sure what I was going to do next. I tried everything

I could do to convince her that her friends and family were crazy, but she wasn't buying it. She asked me to leave. I really had no choice because if she would have called the cops I would have been arrested. I grabbed all my clothes and threw them in a bag and said goodbye. That was the last time I saw her.

Walking down the street with a bag full of clothes is like placing a sign on your back to the police saying come get me. I needed a quick plan, and I had to get off the street before I was arrested. The only thing I could come up with was going into a store and stealing merchandise and trying to return it for cash. I knew that was probably not going to work due to the fact that they stopped giving out cash and gave in store credit instead but it was my only option.

I headed for the department store. Once I got there I stashed my bag of clothes in the back of the building and headed straight for the bathroom. I needed to clean up a little bit. Once I got done cleaning up I headed for the art department. The art department always had expensive pencils, some up to $50 dollars for a set, and they were small and easy to conceal. I stole two sets of pencils and headed for the door. Back when I was stealing to pay my rent I either waited till the next day or returned the merchandise at another store. I never knew if I was being watched so I had to be cautious. But I didn't have till the next day. I needed money now. Once I got out into the parking lot I wondered if I could call the manager of the store and give him some b/s story. I got away with a lot of stuff because of my talking and usually it was when I was most desperate. I guessed it couldn't hurt. I went across the street and used the pay phone. I asked to speak to the manager and once he got on the phone I gave him a story of a lifetime. I explained to him that I was an art student and I had bought these pencils but they were the wrong size and their store didn't carry the size I needed. I also told him that my receipt was back in my dorm room and I didn't have time to go get it. I asked him if he could help me out. He told me that it wasn't a problem and if they would just call him at the return desk he will instruct them what to do. It took about 2 minutes and I walked out with about $106 dollars. This gave me enough money to get a room for 2 nights and something to eat. Now that I had time to think, I needed a plan.

A plan for me consisted of living day to day. I was on the run and I had no money, so it wasn't like I could go out and get an apartment or even buy a car. And the only way I would be able to get around was a car, so I needed to take care of that first. The hotel I was staying at had a dance club on the first floor and one night I decided to go down there and check it out. About an hour into it a girl bought me a drink and started talking to me. I really wasn't into trying to meet someone but she seemed like she was genuine so we started talking. Now this was a little different than the last girl I met. I lied to her because of being out of prison. This girl here I was about to lie to because I was wanted. I told her I was from Alabama and I was up here on business and I would be leaving in a few days. She told me about herself and the rest was just small talk. Once the bar closed down we said our goodbyes and that was that. The next day my hotel phone rings and they tell me I have a guest down in the lobby looking for me. I started to freak. I thought, "Who could this be?" My dad and ex-girlfriend came to mind, or maybe it was the cops or my parole officer. Why wouldn't the cops just come up and get me? Either way I was screwed.

I grabbed as many clothes as I could and headed down the back stairs. Just as I got to the other side of the lobby I saw who it was that was looking for me. It was the girl from the night before. I didn't go right up to her though. I staked out the lobby to make sure she was by herself, and once I saw that she was I went up to her. I asked her how she found me, and she said that she noticed the room number on my key last night and knew my first name was Scott. So she asked them at the desk and they called me. We went and sat over by the door. I still wasn't sure if she was by herself. She wanted to know if I wanted to come to dinner at her parents' house. She figured since I was from out of town that I might need a good home cooked meal. Here I am sitting thinking about what she just asked me. I am a hardened criminal who has been to prison twice and about to go back for a third time and she wants to know if I want to have dinner with her and her family. "Sure," I said, "What time?" She told me she would come pick me up the next night at 6:00 PM. I went back up to my room and thought about what had transpired. I couldn't understand why someone would be so nice and trust worthy. I found out later that she and her family were Christians. That was a word that was very foreign to me. "Oh well," I thought, "I get to eat a good meal."

That night I went back down to the bar that was in the hotel and as I was sitting there having a drink a women came and sat down next to me. I knew this woman. She was staying in the room next to mine and we said "hi" in passing a few times. She was very nice and talkative. She was from California and she was in Michigan on business. I wondered what kind of business because she was 40 years old but looked 60, and she dressed like she was a biker. But it was none of my business so I didn't ask. For the next couple hours we talked about everything and anything. We both said a few different times throughout the conversation that it was real easy to talk to each other. Maybe we had a lot more in common than we thought. She asked me if I wanted to go back to her room. She had something to show me. For some reason I knew she wasn't hitting on me so I agreed.

Once we got up in there she closed the curtains that draped across the window and threw a bag full of crystal meth on the table. She opened it up and took out enough for two lines, one for me and one for her. Crystal meth and cocaine were two of my favorite drugs and I knew that this night was going to be a long one. For the first time in a long time I met someone who I could be completely honest with. I told her everything about me, including being wanted. Her story was she was a drug runner for a biker gang out West and she was making a big delivery up here in Michigan. Obviously the meth that I was snorting was part of that shipment. She went into great detail about her life as a woman in a violent biker gang. She told me stories about how she was the property of the club and whatever they told her to do she did or would risk death. Her sex life consisted of whoever felt like having sex with her in the club and she said she has been beaten so many times she can't even count them anymore. The more meth we did that night the more we talked and before I knew it the sun was coming up. She said, she was checking out in a few hours but before she left she handed me two gifts. The first gift was a few lines of meth to get me through the next day and the second was two $100 bills. She felt bad for me and told me to make sure I get myself a room somewhere for a few days and lay low. We hugged each other and said goodbye. The one person who understood who I was or what I was about just left my life. She left as quickly as she came.

When you do a lot of meth in a short amount of time you can pretty much forget sleeping for a few days. As I looked in the mirror I noticed how blood shot my eyes were. There was no way that I could go to this dinner date looking like this. I needed Visine. The other problem I had and this couldn't be taken care of with Visine, was I needed to calm down. I was running like a million miles an hour. It felt like my heart was about to explode and I couldn't stop grinding the back of my teeth. I needed to sober up a little bit and fast, because she would be there in a few hours. Besides being high and wanted by the police I still had the problem of not having a car. The $200 that women gave me wouldn't last me very long, and I needed a vehicle to get around. But that would have to wait because it was almost time to meet the people who would start the process of changing my life. I took one last look in the mirror and just stared, and then for some reason I remembered the words of the last judge who sent me to prison. He said, "Mr. Mason if you ever come through this court again there will be no more breaks. I will personally see to it that you will get the maximum time allowed by the law." I knew that the next felony conviction meant the possibility of life in prison. Under Michigan law I would now be considered a 4th degree habitual offender. That law meant that the maximum sentence was life in prison. Oh well I thought I am already screwed, so it's time to go out with a bang.

The dinner date I had with this girl's family was very nice. They treated me like I was a member of their family. Of course everything that came out of my mouth was a complete lie but they had no idea. They asked me how I liked Michigan and if there was any place I wanted to go and visit. I said I would just like to drive around and see the sights, "Nothing really in particular." Then the girl who I was with said something that completely shocked me. She told me that she had to work tomorrow and if I wanted, I could drop her off at work and use her car to drive around and check things out, and then pick her up when she was off. The second she said that I thought "Well here is the car I needed." But did I really want to do this to her and her family? Just before we ate dinner this family was praying for me and my trip and even though I didn't believe in this Jesus they were praying to something told me I shouldn't screw with them.

Once dinner was done she took me back to the hotel and told me she would be back in the morning so I could drive her to work. Back in my motel room I took the rest of the meth I had and snorted it. Tomorrow was going to be interesting to say the least. The sun rose up above the curtains in my hotel room and this was the second day I got to see it rise with no sleep in between. The hotel desk called me one last time and told me I had a guest waiting for me. This time I knew who it was. We got into her car and took off for her work place. She told me that she filled up the gas tank and she gave me a map of the city. She also told me that if I got lost I could call her at work and she would get me back to where I needed to be. We pulled up to the side door of her work and when she got out she gave me a hug and said, "Have fun!" in her fun loving sort of way. As I drove off I couldn't believe that I wasn't coming back with her car. I couldn't believe I was about to do this. I went back to the hotel packed up my stuff and got as far away from the city as I could. I knew at about 5:00 PM the cops would be looking for that car. What I didn't know was at about 8:00 PM that night, not only would they be looking for that car but they would also be looking for me, because it didn't take them long to figure out who I really was. Between the hotel knowing my real name and the security surveillance at her work, they put two and two together. I now had another warrant out for my arrest. Could I go for three?

Fourteen
MOST WANTED PART II

I set up shop at a hotel far away from where I just left. I was a good 15 cities away from where I stole that girl's car; and any remorse I had was very short lived. Every day I would go out and steal from stores and call the managers from the store and give them my story as I did before. Some bought into it, others didn't, but I was making enough money to live from day to day that I didn't care if one said no. I started going to a bar down the street from where I was staying and I ended up meeting a waitress at this place. She and I would flirt with each other every night but nothing really came about of it until one night she asked me if I wanted to go to a St. Patrick's party she was hosting. She was house-sitting for a police officer friend of hers and she was having a get together with a bunch of people. I asked her if it would be all cops at this party. She laughed and said, "Well I'm sure there will be some." "Great," I thought, "This is all I need, to hang out at a party with a bunch of police officers." But of course I couldn't turn down the thrill of such an occasion so I agreed.

The night of the party I met her at the bar and left the stolen car I was driving in the parking lot. There was no way in the world I was driving that car to a party full of cops. The night was turning out to be pretty good. Everyone was really cool, and even though a lot of these people were cops I didn't mind it. It's not like they were in uniform, and if I didn't know that they were police officers. I would have never guessed.

About two hours into this party I needed to use the bathroom. When I got in there I noticed a police badge hanging from the other side of the towel rack. It was the cops badge whose house I was in. He was on vacation somewhere out of the country and he didn't need it so that's where he left it I'm assuming. This was too good to pass up. I decided not to steal it yet in case someone noticed, but I did plan on taking it before I left that night. I headed out of the bathroom back to the party. Just before midnight a uniformed police officer who was on duty came over to the house to say hi to everyone. This cop was a real good friend of the girl that invited me and he and I struck up a conversation. I started to ask questions about his job and then I asked him if people are allowed to ride with him as civilians. I wasn't asking if I could ride with him one day, I was just curious. He told me to hang tight he would be back in about 20 minutes. 20 minutes I thought. What is this guy doing? He has to know who I am. He is going to get back up. I needed an escape route just in case and then I thought if he was going to arrest me he would of done it right there and then. My next thought was interrupted when he came back into the house and said, "Are you ready to go?" "Go?" "Yeah, go. You wanted to know if you could tag along so let's go."

I can't even imagine what my face looked like when he said that. I grabbed my jacket and headed out the door. Just before I got into the front seat I thought to myself, "If they ever find out that this police officer was driving around with a convicted felon who was considered armed and dangerous they would have his ass." I got into the front seat and he drove off. We went on a few calls that night. One was in the next city and officers needed help at some big teenage party that was out of control. The call went out that officers needed help and I remember him driving well over 100 mph to get there. The second call was a domestic violence call that was no big deal, and as we were headed back to the house he pulled over someone for having a head light out. Actually this was my call. There were three people in a pickup truck with a headlight out, and I said, "I bet one of those people have warrants. Let's pull them over."

I wanted to see how cops actually ran people's names through their computer system. I got to see firsthand how it all worked. Once we were done he dropped me back off at the house and I thanked him for a great time. He shook my hand. I bet he never would have believed that we would meet again especially in a court room.

Once the party was over, my friend drove me back to the bar to pick up the car I had. Once we turned the corner I saw that it wasn't were I parked it. It was gone. It didn't take long to figure out who had it. I knew no one stole it. The police probably drove by and saw it sitting there and then ran the license plate to see who it belonged to. Once they did that they knew it was stolen.

The girl asked me if I wanted to call the police. I told her no. I said I would deal with it in the morning. I told her thank you for the great evening and headed towards the hotel I was staying at. Once I got into my room I sat down, took off my jacket and pulled something out of my jacket pocket. I just sat there looking at this wondering how I could use it to my advantage. It was the police badge I had stolen from the guy's bathroom. Just before we left I went to use the bathroom and decided to steal it. But before I could use that to my advantage

I needed another car. It wasn't like I could call the police and tell them I needed the car back they just impounded. I needed to know where the closest car dealership was and in the drawer of the night stand was my answer. I stayed up for the rest of the night looking through that phone book trying to plot my next move.

"Can I help you?" the salesmen asked when I walked through the door. I said, "Sure I'm looking to buy a car today. Can you show me what you have?" We sat down at his desk and he informed me that he had only been selling cars for two weeks and asked if I could be patient with him if he didn't have all the answers. We took about 10 minutes and talked about what I liked and then he went off to grab the keys to the cars so we could look inside them. I purposely chose 6 cars because that meant he would have multiple sets of keys and when you have multiple sets of keys you tend to forget which is which. We went out to the parking lot and looked over all the cars that I requested, and once we were done we went back to his desk. I told him that I liked two of them but I wasn't sure. I asked him if he had any brochures on these cars. Just before he got up, he put all six keys on the desk and went to go get the brochures. I turned around to make sure he was gone and once he was, I stole one of the keys. This guy had so much stuff on his desk, and on top of the keys he had for the cars I was looking at he also had others keys to other cars. I knew he wouldn't miss this key for awhile. He came back and handed me the brochures to the cars I asked about. I told him I would be back later that day to purchase one. I think he was so excited to sell a car he never even noticed that the key was gone. It took me about 30 seconds to get to the car I had the key for. I opened the door took one more look around and drove off. It doesn't get any crazier than this I thought. I just drove a $25,000 car off the lot right in front of everybody, and just in case you are keeping count this would be felony warrant number three. There was no doubt who stole this car. They had cameras all over the place and on top of that they had a photo copy of my driver's license. I needed to get out of the city limits before they caught me. I needed to go somewhere that was familiar to me. I was headed back to where I grew up.

Once I got into a hotel, I had to put a new plan into action. I knew that the police badge I had would come into play but in order to act like a cop I needed a gun like a cop. I didn't need a real one I just needed something that looked like one. I remember seeing the pellet guns at a store once, and they looked just like a real 40 Glock. Sometime later Federal law made the makers of these guns put orange paint on the end of the barrels so police officers would know they weren't real. The one I bought didn't have that orange tip and it looked real. I have never robbed someone with a gun or anything like that and this wasn't going to change. What I had in mind with the badge and gun was to be able to return the items I stole from stores without having a receipt. As I said before, if you can't trust a cop who can you trust? My plan was to go into the paint department at these stores and steal 4 or 5 paint brushes that were worth $25 a piece and then I would actually buy a couple gallons of cheap paint and a few rollers and go to the next store and return them. I had a receipt for the paint and rollers that I bought but not for the paint brushes. When they asked me about the receipt for the paint brushes, I told them that my wife had the receipt and she was at work and I was on my lunch hour and didn't have time to go and get the receipt from her. In order for them to return $100 in paint brushes they needed a manager's approval. Once the manager came to the return desk, he saw the badge that I had hanging from my neck and he also saw the gun, so he automatically assumed that I was a police officer. With me being a cop or so they thought and also having the receipts for other paint products, they always approved the return. They never questioned it. I was able to make enough money for me to stay somewhere for a few days and not have to worry about where I would be tomorrow. The extra money I had went towards partying. I started hanging out at a few different bars and I started doing meth and coke again, "My long lost friends," I always said. They were the only things that made me feel good, and I needed a lot of them.

Having people think that I was a cop made me feel like the drugs did. It made me feel good about myself. It made me feel like I was somebody even though it was all a lie. People looked at me differently. It was like I had some magic powers or something. One night as I was getting ready to go out I decided that I was going to play the cop game. I was going to go to the bar with the badge around my neck. I figured this would impress some people there. All I was doing that night was going to eat so it wasn't like I was going to be drinking. Having a police officer eating in a bar wasn't a big deal I thought so off I went. Once I got to the front door there was a bouncer sitting there and he asked me for ID. I said, "Sure. No problem." I unzipped my jacket, and before I could get my ID out he saw the police badge. He said, "Sorry officer, go right in." Before I did, though, he asked me if I was there on pleasure or business." I said, "Pleasure" and he smiled. This

116

bar was a little shady, so I'm assuming having cops in there wasn't something new to them.

This place was more of a bar than a restaurant, so I had to find a seat way in the back because there were people dancing and hanging out in the front. I found a good seat and sat down. Once I took my jacket off and probably because of the bouncer telling people I was a cop, I had everybody looking at me. My waitress kept on calling me officer and she was the best waitress I had ever had. I'm sure the rest of the bar didn't think so but I did. Even though I wasn't a cop I saw how people treated them. My waitress probably thought if she was super polite that one day I might return the favor. Maybe I would let her out of a ticket or something, who knows, but I loved the treatment I was receiving. Once I was done with dinner I decided to shoot some pool and I asked if I could have the next game. Everybody that was standing there was just staring at me, probably because most of them were either high or had drugs on them.

I assured the ones who were standing by me that I was only here to eat dinner and shoot a little pool not to arrest anybody. I also explained to them that I was on call so if I had to leave in the middle of a game they would understood why. I had this all down pat. I was truly as I had for so many years living something I was not and could never become. If they only knew the truth I thought. I am wanted by the whole damn state on countless warrants and there is probably an award for whoever turns me in. Screw it I thought. I am having a good time. My good time clouded my judgment though, just as it always had throughout my life.

I was just about to take a shot on the pool game I was playing when someone whispered in my ear, "Are you an undercover police officer?" I turned to see who was asking the question and I didn't recognize the face. I thought about the question for a second and I said, "No I am not." I knew who was asking the question. I knew because they used the word police officer. Anybody from this bar would have either said cop or 5-0, but not police officer. The second I said, "No," this man bounced my head off the pool table and had me bent over it. Out of the corner of my eye I saw other people running toward me with their guns drawn shouting at people to get down. It was like a movie. Once they searched me and took the badge I had around my neck, they decided it was safe to take me out. One police officer kept on saying, "Where is the gun? We know you have a gun! Where is it?" "I'm telling him I don't have a gun." "Yes you do mother f*****! Give it to us. Give us the gun or I am going to whip your punk ass right here." I told him and the other 20 officers to go screw themselves. Once they were convinced I didn't have a gun they took me out of the bar.

Now any time I have ever been arrested, the police would handcuff me in the back and walk me out. This time they did handcuff me in the back but instead of walking me out they dragged me out. They dragged me all across that bar to show people inside the bar they meant business, and also because they were pissed at me for stealing a police officer's badge. Once we got outside I saw the seriousness of what had just transpired. There were cops everywhere. They had two major intersections closed off and police officers from 5 different agencies were in the parking lot. They must have thought that they had the boss of a major crime family. What I didn't know but soon found out was a waitress in the bar knew who I truly was. She called 911 and told them my name and also told them I was impersonating a police officer. They asked her if I had a gun and she said she thought I did. That's all it took. Till this day I have no idea who that waitress was. I asked one of the detectives a few days later but they feared that I might try to do something to her, so they wouldn't tell me. Her name was also blacked out from my court transcripts.

The city jail that they put me in for that night was right across the street from where I was arrested. There were so many different warrants out for my arrest I don't think they knew where to start. Because I was a parole violator they had every right to put me in jail without charging me, but they needed to call my parole officer so he could violate my parole. At about 4:30 in the morning I heard over the loud speaker in my cell, "Mason you've got a visitor." "A visitor? Who is visiting me at 4:30 in the morning?" I thought. They led me into this small room that had a metal table with two metal stools and they told me to sit down. From where I was sitting I could see all the way down the hall way and once he walked through the door I knew who my visitor was. It was my parole officer. "Great," I thought, "this is going to be a long morning."

Just before he sat down he reminded me of what he told me and my dad the first time I saw him in his office. I wasn't amused by his comments, and besides I knew I was going back to prison for a very long time; so I told him where he could stick his comments. He got the last laugh though. He handed me a sheet of paper and told me I could either sign it or not. It really didn't matter to him. I looked at the paper and I already knew what it was for. It was my parole violation notification. It listed the charges that I was being charged with 1-10. I asked him how do you have 10 different charges against me and he just smiled. I knew right then and there that I was done. The next time I get out of prison I will be getting social security I thought, and I was serious.

Fifteen

SIX HOURS ON A CROSS

Within a few days of my arrest I was back in prison. The prison I ended up in was strictly for parole violators. Once you violated your parole you would have to go back in front of the parole board and they would figure out then what they were going to do with you. Some guys went back on the street and others would get sent to a place they called TRV. TRV was a 90 day program from hell and nobody ever wanted to end up there, but it was only 90 days compared to the two years at a time some guys where getting. Because I had so many charges pending in court the parole board gave me a two year continuance. They wanted to make sure that I didn't get out before all my court dates. They also knew that I was probably going to end up with a 10 or 15 year sentence, and once that happened I would not be underneath their jurisdiction anymore. Either way the prison system had me for awhile.

Not knowing what is going to happen to you has probably got to be the worst feeling in the world. Whether you're in prison or not, uncertainty is a rough way to live. In my case uncertainty lay in the hands of many judges and prosecutors. Because I had so many cases in so many different cities it seemed like I spent more time in court rooms than I did in prison. My first court date was in the city that I stole the police badge. The prosecutor for obvious reasons wanted my butt to burn so he decided to charge me with three different crimes, all stemming for one stolen police badge.

Once I got into court it wasn't a pretty sight. Every single cop in the city was in the court room that morning or it seemed like it anyhow. You would have thought the way they were looking at me that I just killed a police officer. I guess stealing a police badge was almost as bad. Before the judge could start the proceedings, my lawyer needed to be there and he was nowhere to be found. The court system must provide an attorney for you if you cannot afford one, and I obviously couldn't afford one; so it was their job to make sure I had one. About 10 minutes went by and the judge was about to postpone the case when a man in a real nice suit spoke up on my behalf. He asked the judge if he could have a minute with me. The man introduced himself to me. He was an attorney from a very prestige law firm downtown, and he asked me if he could defend me in this case.

I said, "Excuse me?" with shock written all over my face. "Sir I couldn't afford 2 minutes of your time let alone a whole court case." He told me don't worry about all that and then stood up and faced the judge. "Your honor, Mr. Mason has retained me in these proceedings and I would like a few minutes with my client in private." The judge accepted the man's motion, and off I went into a private room with my new lawyer. The first thing I noticed about him was the Rolex watch he had on his wrist. The thing probably cost as much as a car. He must be doing something right I thought. "The reason why I am taking your case is because I was sitting here waiting on my client to show up and then I noticed that you had no attorney. Something kept on telling me that I needed to defend you." "Something?" I said. "What, are you hearing voices?" He said, "It's just something I feel I need to do." "Number two," he said, "I hate the prosecutor that is assigned to handle your case and I was reading the charges that they had against you I noticed that he screwed up so this is my chance to stick it to his ass. I laughed and said, "Good, then stick it to him." "When we get out there I want you to shut your mouth and let me do the talking," he said. I just shook my head in agreement.

That three second walk from the room I was just in to the court room seemed like forever. I had no idea what was going to happen and I wasn't too sure if this lawyer was on the up and up but what choice did I have. The judge called the court into session and said let's begin. "Your honor," my lawyer said, "Mr. Mason has been charged with 3 separate cases stemming from one incident. Two of these counts are for being in possession of a stolen police badge. How many police badges did he steal? There is only one badge in question here your honor. Secondly, your honor, these three cases that my client has been charged with are small in comparison with what he is facing in other courts. My client has two other cases that carry life sentences, and I would hate to have to spend the court's time arguing that he is being charged unfairly in your court." The judge looked intrigued and asked my lawyer what he had in mind. "Your honor" he said, "My client has been in prison for 14 days now and he has a minimum sentence from the parole board of two years, and that is not including the other charges against him. We would be willing to plead guilty to these three charges involving the badge if you were willing to give him time served." The judge looked at the prosecutor and asked him if he objected to this. "No your honor" he said, "that will be fine." My lawyer shook my hand and said, "Good luck, Scott." As I was being led out of the court room one of the police officers from that city said, "If we ever see you in our city again we are going to bust your ass." "Whatever", I said. The whole ride back to the prison I was trying to figure out what had just happened. I thought for sure I was going to get nailed for the police badge. "I guess the gods are looking out for me," I thought.

A month or so went by from that court date and I had a lot of uncertainty about my future. I had two more court dates and those were for the two cars I had stolen. Both cases were in counties that were known for handing out a lot of prison time for people like myself who kept on screwing up. Just as I was in deep thought about that, I was interrupted by a friend of mine who asked me if I wanted to go to the prison chapel that night to hear a guy speak. He had been locked up in prison but now he had turned his life around for Jesus. I looked at him and said, "Are you out of your mind? Why in the hell would I want to go there?" He said, "Okay, I was just asking. Settle down."

When he left I went back to thinking about my court cases but for some reason I couldn't get this chapel thing out of my mind. One of the reasons I really didn't want to go was because everyone who would be attending would be black. Well everyone but my friend and I. Even though I had only been back in the prison system for a short time I was still a gang member and at this time the gang I was a part of was going to war with the black gangs in other prisons. I thought for sure if I went to this chapel I would be set up to get stabbed. Gangs inside the prison system didn't have any morals so to hit someone in a church really didn't matter. Another reason I didn't want to go was because I just didn't care about this guy Jesus my friend was always talking about. This guy wouldn't shut up about him. We would eat together all the time and he would talk about how Jesus loved me and so on. I seriously got sick of it, and besides I always wondered if this Jesus guy was so great why do you keep on coming back to prison.

That night at dinner time my friend asked me one last time if I wanted to go. He said, "What are you going to do tonight, sit in your cell?" He had a good point. "Okay," I said, "I will go, but if I get stabbed and live I am going to kick your ass." He assured me I would not get stabbed. After dinner I washed up and headed to my friend's cell. "Time to go," I said. He grabbed his Bible and smiled.

As we walked into the prison chapel that night I didn't really know what to expect. I always heard how black people would praise this Jesus guy. They would be jumping up and down and jamming to some Christian music. I caught a glimpse of this one time when I was in Jackson prison and I thought how stupid it was. But this time around in this chapel it was just the opposite. Everyone just kind of took their seats. When the "show" as I called it got going, the man who came to speak started talking to us about how he to once was locked up in prison and how he was addicted to crack cocaine. The more he talked the louder he got and before I knew it, everybody was on their feet screaming, "Thank you!" to Jesus. "Thank you Jesus for what?" I thought. Before he continued on he wanted everyone who wasn't standing to stand up so we could pray. He said he felt like God was telling him to pray. I didn't want to look like an outcast so I stood also. Before He started to pray he went on talking about how he found Jesus in a place just like this and how Jesus loved us so much that he died on the cross for you and when he said that it was like he was just talking to me. When he said that Jesus loves us so much I had tears running down my face. I didn't even know that though because I was engulfed in something I can only explain as Christ's love.

It was like He was holding on to me and the tighter He held me the more I cried. The man who was running the service got all excited and said, "See, that's what I'm talking about, that man back there is being touched by God." Instead of him praying he started singing and the band that was there followed suit. I stood there for what seemed like eternity and I started singing with everyone else. I didn't know the words but I tried and as I sang I felt what can only be described as the greatest gift anyone could ever get and that was peace. Every single thing that weighed on my mind for so many years was gone. It was like I was a brand new person inside. It honestly felt like someone lifted a thousand pounds of bricks off of me all at one time. What took years to build up in my life was gone in a second.

I wish I could describe this better but I just can't. How do I describe something as powerful as the living God coming down to a prison in the middle of nowhere just to introduce Himself to me? I can't. Once chapel was over the man who came to speak hugged me and said, "Your life will never be the same. I love you brother." A black man was hugging me and calling me brother. "This must be God," I thought. On our way back to the housing block all I could think about is what just happened to me. Was it real? I had no way of knowing. I think it's like winning the lottery you don't really believe it until you pick up the check. That night I thought about the lawyer who helped me with the police badge charges. Was that God who did that? It had to have been. The next morning I woke up I felt great, but the feeling I had was gone. I didn't feel that love I did the night before so I set out to find out why.

"Dude, what the heck?" I said to my friend. "What happened to how I felt last night? It's not there anymore." He explained to me that having a relationship with Jesus is not a feeling, it's so much more. He said, "You were touched by God, and now you need to learn about who Jesus is, what he's about, why He died on the cross and why He rose from the grave." "Well who is going to teach me that?" I asked. He handed me a Bible. "John is", he said. But before John could teach me anything I heard my name over the loud speaker. "Mason, pack your stuff up and report to the officers' station."

They told me that I was headed to court and I needed to go sit in the visiting room until they came and got me. Two hours later I was headed down the street in a police car and as I looked back at the prison I thought they might be able to take my freedom, but they can't take what away how I felt last night. Bring on the judge.

Sixteen

SIN'S GOT A PRICE

I had to sit in a one man cell all weekend until I could see the judge on Monday. At this point I was already back in my prison mode of just give me a pillow and a blanket and leave me alone. But the cells at the city jail didn't offer me the leave me alone feel I was looking for. The city I was in was known for all its bars, which meant a lot of people who got arrested on the weekend where probably drunk, and this Saturday night was no exception. As the night went on I had to listen to all these drunk people cry and scream at the top of their lungs how they want their phone call or how they were set up and then usually the crying mode would set in. Some of these guys cried like little babies. They told anyone who would listen how sorry they were. Many times throughout the night I would scream down the hall and tell them to shut up. It was miserable. I couldn't wait to get back to prison.

When Monday morning rolled around I had a visitor. She introduced herself as my court appointed attorney. Once she said her last name I said, "Hey my judge has the same last name." She said, "I know he's my dad." I looked up at ceiling in my cell and said, "Thank you." She probably thought I was crazy, but I was looking past that ceiling. I was looking toward Heaven or the little bit I knew about it. She said, "Now look, they have you on the car you stole from the girl. They have the video from the cameras that were at her work and it shows you dropping her off. They also have the hotel clerk who will testify that she picked you up that morning. There is really no way out of this. I talked to the prosecutor on this case and he offered you a deal." "Great," I thought, "what is the deal?" Seven years in prison instead of ten?" But she said, "If you plead guilty, he will give you a 345 day sentence that will run concurrent with your parole board sentence of two years." What that meant was that while I was serving two years for my parole violation I would also be serving this 345 day sentence at the same time. I took the offer

She said "I thought you would," with a smile. She also went on to say she wasn't too sure why I was getting this gift from the prosecutor. "But if I were you," she said, "I would seriously think about a career change because if you ever come back through this court again, I can promise you that they will throw the book at you." I went in front of the judge that day and he told me the same thing my lawyer did. He sentenced me to the 345 days just as we agreed upon and back to prison I went.

On the way back I thought about the next court that I had to go to. This court was notorious throughout the state for handing down boat loads of prison time. Most of the judges had nicknames that inmates would give them, and they weren't good. I thought for sure that I would get a minimum of 5 years out of this court, and as a matter of fact the lawyer I just had asked me about that. She said "You have to go in front of this certain judge don't you?" You know that's not good, right? He is going to nail you to the wall Scott." I thanked her for the warning.

Once I got back to the prison, I was excited to tell my friend what had happened. He was excited for me and he was also excited for another reason. The parole board had decided to let him go home and in two days. I would lose the only person I knew who could teach me about the Bible, Jesus, and everything I needed to know about what happened that night in chapel. It didn't matter though, because the next day I would be packing up once again. It was time to go to court one last time. "Man," I thought, "can't these people give me a break?"

That night my friend gave me the brief history about Jesus. He showed me how the Bible would change my life, and he highlighted a few verses for me. He said, "Take this Bible wherever you go." It was time to lockdown in our cells for the night. We hugged each other and said goodbye. He would be going home in a few hours, and I would be going to court. Two different paths, but as he put it, we would see each other again. I never did see him again, but he wasn't talking about on earth. He was talking about Heaven.

The court appointed lawyer I had in this case was a lot different than the others I had had. First of all, she was very blunt and to the point, and secondly she never even read my file. I knew that lawyers hated doing pro bono work. They had to do a certain amount of pro bono cases a year and they just went through them as fast as they could. They had paying clients lined up, and they were taking time away from them to help someone like me. I knew that she never looked at my file because when she sat me down she said, "Look Mr. Mason, you are screwed here. They have video from the car dealership where you stole that car from. It shows you walking out of the dealership and getting right into the car and then you driving off. It's pretty open and shut for the prosecutor. You are going to have to do some time on this case." She said, and I swear to this day I will never forget it, "I can get you six months in the county jail. I'm sorry but that's the best I can do."

I asked her point blank if she had talked to the prosecutor already about this. She said she had. "And he is going along with this?" She said, "I have the plea agreement right here from the prosecuting attorney's office. If you accept theses terms sign here. Once we get in front of the judge he will ask you..." I stopped her in mid sentence. "Ma'am," I said, "I know the drill, but what you are telling me cannot be correct." "Why is that?" she asked. I said, "Do you realize that I am sentenced to prison for two years already?" She said that she didn't. That's how I knew she hadn't read my file. I said, "They can't sentence me to 6 months in the county jail. My prison time supersedes any time this court can give me, so quit screwing around with me and start acting like you actually care and actually read my files." She said, "I will be back," and she left.

I was so pissed off. Here I'm about to possibly get sentenced to God knows what and this lady could care less. I was just another number to her, just like the prison system. About 20 minutes later she came back and said, "You are right. I'm sorry. I can't get that deal for you." "No crap," I said. "I'm not even a lawyer and I knew that. Where in the hell did you go to law school?" She said, "Mr. Mason, if you would let me finish and quit being a smart ass I will tell you that the 6 months in the county jail is still on the table, but you would have to do it after the parole board releases you from prison. What do you think of that?" I almost kissed her. "Now," she said, "You can get another lawyer and get sent up for 10 years, or you can stick with me, shut your mouth, and thank me later." "Yes ma'am," I said. "That's what I thought," she shot back with a smile.

I went into court that day with a new lease on life. I had no more court dates after this one and the 10 plus years I thought I would get turned into only 2 ½ years. After my two years were up with the parole board I still had to go back in front of them to see if they would release me. They could technically keep me for 8 ½ more years because that's what my maximum sentence was on the stolen car that got me sent to prison the second time. I guess I would have to leave it in God's hands. He had been with me this far. Why would he stop now? I still didn't know anything about Him but that was about to change. God was about to hear from me, and it wasn't going to be good.

Seventeen

HELL ON EARTH (4 BLOCK)

Once I got back to prison I knew it was just a matter of time before they rode me out to another prison now that I was sentenced and had no more cases. I had a few things going against me though. The way my file read was I had to go to the county jail after I was done serving my time in prison. So that automatically put me into a higher security and also my gang affiliation even stepped that up higher. The Department of Corrections implemented a program that if they knew you were known to be a gang member then they would put you on what is known as a Security Threat Group list. And that always made your security level go higher. So with all this against me, I could only pray that I would be sent to a half way decent prison. And that's exactly what I started to do, pray.

Since Jackson prison was in the process of closing completely they were sending the worst of the worst from there to a prison in Muskegon called Muskegon Correctional Facility, or MCF for short. The state also put most of the gang leaders in MCF so they could monitor all the gang leader's activities from one place. Everyone who was in prison knew that the worst prison to go to in the state was MCF. Now I know that sounds crazy that someone would prefer a certain prison over another but trust me, there are some prisons you just don't want to end up in; and once again MCF was one of those places.

As my transfer was drawing closer, I prayed every hour on the hour that I wouldn't be sent to MCF. I actually found verses in the Bible that had to do with God giving me what I asked for. So I stood on those verses. One morning I heard over the loud speaker, "Mason report to the officers' station." I looked up towards Heaven and said, "Alright Lord if you are real like I believe you are, then you need to hook me up... anywhere but MCF." I went to the officer's station and they told me I was being transferred. I asked them, "Where am I going?" but I knew they wouldn't tell me until I got onto the prison bus for security reasons. I went back to my cell packed my stuff and headed towards the sally port where we would be shackled and sent on our way. There were about 6 other guys with me, and once we were on the bus the Officer started calling out names and telling each person the prison to which they were going. I was the fourth one on the list and he said, "Mason you are going to MCF."

This next conversation was the actual conversation I had with God. I said, "Are you freaking kidding me? You come into my life and change everything about me and now you're doing this?" I was so pissed off for the next hour or so I just sat there staring out the window, and then something hit me. I knew that MCF was bad. I knew about all the violence that occurred there every single day. I had even heard about how the state somehow sent all the homosexuals to MCF. But I also had heard about one particular housing block at MCF, and that was "4 Block." Basically this block was the worst of the worst state wide. I heard stories about how "4 Block" was considered the Wild West. Once I realized this, I started praying again. "Alright Lord you can redeem yourself here. Obviously you weren't paying attention when they sent me here so please pay attention now. I can live with MCF, but please make sure they don't send me to this "4 Block." There are 5 other blocks in this prison that you can send me to. Please Lord please." I wondered if He was listening.

Once an inmate arrives at MCF they are placed in 1 block for two weeks. In these two weeks you go through a classification process, and they want to see if you will be able to handle this prison. Once this process is complete, they send you to a Permanente block. The first few days I was there I pretty much kept to myself. I didn't know anyone and I wanted to keep it that way for awhile. I figured if I could just keep low I might be able to get through these next couple of years with no problem. I also knew that I needed to learn more about God, but I wasn't sure how. I guessed church services would be a good start. So I set off to find out about what type of services they had there.

One day while I was walking on the yard, I saw two guys studying what appeared to be the Bible. I went up to them and asked them when church was held around there. What I found out kind of shocked me. This dump of a prison had some of the best church services throughout the prison system! They had people come in from the streets every Sunday and the Chaplin there really cared about the inmates. They said, "Even the correctional staff encourages inmates to go on Sundays." Then they told me about the band. Some guy who had a famous band in the streets ran the worship part of the service. I asked who that was. I was surprised that I knew the name. I always wondered what had happened to him. He was convicted of murder years ago and now he was leading worship in prison.

"Money and fame can't even keep someone out of prison," I thought. I asked what time the service started, and they said 6:30 PM on Sundays. I told them I would be there. As Sunday was fast approaching I still was praying about not being sent to "4 Block." Now that I was here the stories people told were only the half of it. Every single day since I had been there something was going on in "4 Block." One day two guys got stabbed. Another day they had Michigan State police drug dogs going through the cells. It seemed it was just one thing after the next. I figured I really need to get to this church service. Maybe God would listen to me there.

As I walked into the auditorium where Sunday's service was being held, I automatically felt like I was back in high school. This was exactly what the auditorium would look like in any high school across the country. As a matter of fact the whole prison looked like a college campus. When MCF was built it was strictly for inmates who were considered "honor inmates," so it was the nicest prison in the whole state. Everything about it showed that it was once used for this purpose. It still had that look but the inmates that were here now where anything but, "honor inmates". I grabbed a seat in the back and settled in for the show. The band started playing and to be honest they were even better than those guys said they were. I was very impressed. Growing up Catholic, this type of worship was new to me. The lead singer was jumping up and down screaming how much he loves God. The drummer, guitarist and bassist all followed suit and were jamming as loud as they could. Once they were done the lead singer said a prayer like I never heard before and told everyone that was there that night to, "Greet someone around you." "Oh great," I thought, "now I have to talk to these people."

The first guy that came up to me was a guy named Rex. Rex was about 6'3" and weighed about 230 pounds. He didn't look like someone you would see in a prison service like this, but something in his demeanor and eyes said different. We talked for a few minutes and the guy who was preaching started the service. I really don't remember what he talked about, but I knew I liked it. It was different than what the priest on Sunday morning mass would do. Once he was done and wrapped it up, it was time to go back to our housing blocks. But just before I did, Rex told me to meet him on the yard the next morning so we could talk more. I asked him what block he was in. He said, "4 Block."

I couldn't meet with Rex on the yard that day because I had to move to my new block. My time was up in 1 block. "Mason pack up your stuff and come to the officers' station," I heard over the loud speaker. The whole time I was packing I was reminding God of our agreement. "Now look," I said, "You already screwed me once by sending me to this dump. Please don't let them send me to 4 Block." As I approached the station, the officer said to report to 4 Block and see officer so and so they will assign you to your new cell. I said, "I'm going to 4 Block?" and he just looked at me like I was stupid. Again he said, "Go to 4 block-" I cut him off in mid sentence. "I heard you," I said and grabbed my things and headed over there. I thought maybe I heard him wrong so I had to make sure.

I thought long and hard about writing what I told God on that walk over to 4 Block but I am going to only say this, it wasn't good. I am embarrassed even to this day that I would talk to Him the way I did, but I did learn in that conversation that He loves us no matter what, and what I told Him wasn't like something no one ever said that to Him before. He knows our hearts and that is the key. My heart wasn't saying screw you, my mouth was; and it would be something He would need to work on.

As I walked into my new block, I knew right off the bat that this block was different from the one I just came from. It was loud. It smelled of stale liquor which I will get into later, and people were hanging all over the place. 1 Block had a rule that you couldn't hang out in front of someone's cell. Here in 4 Block I think the rule was 5 people couldn't hang out in front of someone's cell, because every cell had at least 4 people in front of it. Honestly, the place looked like Hell on earth. But there was nothing I could do.

Once the officer gave me my cell number I headed up towards the second gallery. I passed by a few people I had sat with at chow or seen on the yard but nobody I really knew, and then I heard someone call my name. But it wasn't my real name; it was my gang nickname. So much for laying low I thought. The guy who called me was a gang member of the gang I was in and he and I first met each other years ago. I actually liked this guy and it was kind of cool seeing him again. We talked for a few minutes and then he started telling me about what was going on around there. He told me how every gang leader was there and the violence was out of control. He told me that the officers cared about one thing around there, and that was going home when their shift was up.

That meant that as long as they didn't have to do paperwork, they didn't care what we did. That goes back to the whole block smelling like liquor thing. Quite a few inmates had homemade alcohol brewing in their cells, and you could smell that crap a mile away. Some of these guys even had stills set up in their cells. I found out real quickly that officers really didn't care too much what was going on because one day some guy passed out by my cell and it was count time. One of the officers who was counting passed by the guy that was on the floor and counted him just as if he was in a cell. I just shook my head.

This block and the officers reminded me a lot of an NFL football game. In a NFL game the referees usually only throw flags for penalties when it's absolute necessary, and this place was no exception. Once I got settled in my cell and put all my stuff away I grabbed my soap and towel and headed for the shower. Taking a shower in this place proved to be a challenge. I didn't know that there were certain times during the day that homosexuals would turn their tricks in the shower area. It was usually between shift change for the officers and I happened to be taking a shower pretty much close to shift change. I walked in on two guys having sex and turned around and walked out. The shower would have to wait.

Throughout my years there it was hard to figure out when guys were using the shower for their own personal pimp fest, so basically you just dealt with them screwing around with each other. You got in and got out in quick fashion. That was just a minor challenge compared to figuring out on a daily basis who was really your friend in prison. I was a member of a powerful gang and with that I had a lot of people on my side,

139

but they were only on my side when it fit their agenda. It was time to figure out what that agenda was.

Being involved with a prison gang has its advantages and disadvantages. The advantage is power in numbers. The more people you had backing you, the less likely people would mess with you; but in our case we had less members than any other gang in the prison and we were considered the ones you just didn't mess with. Being a gang member this time around was a little different for me than when I first went to prison. I was older now and I already had done quite a few years in prison up to this point and even though I knew at some point I would be going home, I still had the attitude screw with me and I will kill you. The disadvantages are numerous. For starters the gang came first. Nothing else mattered in your life but them. If you had a visit coming from the outside world and one of the ranking members told you to cancel that visit then you canceled that visit and you better not ask why. If an order came from the top to kill the warden then you better do whatever it takes to get to that warden and kill him or they will come after you. The only thing that mattered to these guys was power and money and nothing would stand in their way of having both.

Every day we would have meetings on the yard and we would discuss what was going on in the prison and who needed to be dealt with. The problem with having, let's say 200 guys, is at least one of those 200 will get into some kind of trouble every single day. If they were in trouble then we were in trouble, because they represented us. Over time, I became real good at stopping trouble before it happened. Most of the ranking members of other gangs lived in the block I did so I decided that I needed to become friends with these guys to a point. I always had respect for them and they had respect for me so if a problem arose they would come to me first before going out and handling it with some type of violence. This wasn't always the case though. One of the members of our gang decided to get into a fight with a rival gang member from the West coast. The West coast guy was at least twice the size of him and with one punch the fight was over.

In normal circumstances a guy will fight one on one and if he loses then he loses and that's the end of it. This is not the case, however, when it comes to two different gang members going at it. The one guy who lost embarrassed us, and he needed to take care of this or he was going to be taken care of by us.

As I said they are only your friends until their agenda takes over. If word got out that we were soft then every gang would try to take over what we were doing and that would mean an all out war. This guy eventually got back at the West coast guy in one of the most violent ways I have ever seen in my life. They beat him with rakes, baseball bats and punched and kicked him until he was unrecognizable. The thing I never got was right after this happened, and I mean within 3 minutes, every guy that was involved with this beating was caught and eventually charged with attempted murder. This problem was taken care of when the guy got beat fair and square but because of the gangs image it had to go farther. Lives are forever changed and ruined because of something so ridiculous and you can even take it a step further and look outside of the prison walls and fences. Some of these guys had children and now because of an image they might not ever see their dads again. I wish I could say that after this day I would have just got out but in the gang world there is no such thing.

Once you're in you are in for life, and I had a lot of years left on my sentence and I just couldn't take the chance of being on my own. Besides I was about to get promoted. I would soon become a ranking gang member and as crazy as this sounds, it was God that would do the promoting.

Eighteen
GOD TIME NOW

Living a few cells away from me was the guy I met at the first Sunday night church service I attended at MCF. I obviously didn't know it then, but Rex would be the biggest influence I ever had in my life on so many different levels. We became quick friends, and one day while walking the yard I got to hear his story and why he is so at peace even though he will probably never get out of prison. Growing up Rex was learning how to become a Jehovah's Witness. That consisted of knowing their Bible from beginning to end without exception and basically how to get people to come to religion. He said it was like being a car salesman. Once he was of age and had the knowledge that they expected of him, they sent him out knocking on doors and telling anyone who would listen what it meant to be a JW. Somewhere along that line though it went bad for him, and he started hanging around the wrong crowd and eventually got addicted crack cocaine.

One day he and his friend went to a local drug dealer to buy a few rocks (crack) and while he waited in the car his friend went in and robbed the dealer. Something went wrong with the robbery and his friend shot and killed the dealer. A few days later Rex was arrested and charged with murder. Even though he didn't pull the trigger, he knew about the crime and didn't turn his friend into the police. What happened though once he got to prison was a life changing process not only for him but everyone he has helped since then. Somewhere along the line he seen that the JW religion was not only wrong but it had brain washed him into thinking they were the only way and everyone else was going to hell. One night he asked God to show him what the truth was and he said God did. I never asked him how God revealed the truth to him but whatever it was it was powerful enough for Rex to be at peace with a life prison sentence, and that was good enough for me.

Rex started to take me on as a full time student. That meant that he would literally sink everything he knew about Christianity and life into me. We started reading the Bible together every chance we had. We would go to lunch and dinner together and we would study while we were waiting to eat. We literally talked about the Bible and nothing else for a few months. One day at dinner he handed me a catalog from a place called Christian Book Distributors. It had page after page of every kind of reading material you could get on Christianity. They sold commentaries, concordances, Bibles, Christian living books and so on. I remember looking at this and asking him, "Why so many books?" Up to this point all we did was study the Bible and I thought that was good enough. He highlighted a few books in there that he wanted me to get and he said if I couldn't pay for them then he would buy them for me.

I was pretty excited to get these books but in order to get them I needed my grandpa to buy them for me. I knew no one else in my family would and besides, I didn't have that kind of money in my prison account. I said, "Alright Lord, if you want me to have these than you need to tell my grandpa because I just don't think he will buy them for me." The next day I called my grandpa and told him exactly what I wanted and why I needed them. "Sure, no problem," he said. "I will call them when I'm done on the phone with you." "Thank you Lord," I said once I hung up. But I'll be honest, I didn't have the first clue as to what I was thanking him for because once I got these books delivered to me I started to look them over and was more confused than ever.

I went down to Rex's cell and said, "Can you please tell me why you feel the need to teach about Jew's and their history." I had ordered a book on the Jewish Feast's and lifestyle back in Jesus' day. He explained to me that Jesus was a Jew and then he went on to talk about the differences between Jews and Gentiles. I walked away from his cell thinking, "Man, here I thought I knew something about Christ and I know nothing." I was pretty discouraged to be honest because I thought I was getting good at something. It excited me to call family members and tell them I was really learning about Jesus and the Bible. The funny thing though is if one of my family members asked me a question about the Old Testament I would have replied, "What's that?" Rex and I for the last few months had only studied out of the New Testament. We studied strictly about Jesus and his apostles but that was about to change.

One day while I was reading by myself I came across something that didn't sound right to me. The Bible was contradicting itself and at that moment I knew it had all been a lie. I knew this crap was too good to be true. I jumped up from my bed and headed out the door toward Rex's cell. I was going to tell him where he could shove this Bible and his friendship but I was side tracked by a fellow gang member. He said, "We have an emergency meeting in 10 minutes on the yard." Great, someone either has died or is about to get killed. This was going to be a long day.

When a whole gang meets on the yard everyone knows something is up and that includes the correctional officers. As I was heading to the yard I overheard one of the officers over his walkie-talkie say that they are meeting on the East side of the yard. All available officers please report to the East side of the yard. I knew this had to be big. Somebody got killed and now we are going to war I thought. Once I got out there I found out why we were there. One of the highest ranking members spoke up and said, "So and so, the Chief of Security got into a fight and he is in the hole. They are transferring him to a different prison. As of now Scott is the new Chief of Security." Before I could speak up everyone shook my hand and we all went our separate ways. In prison we were only allowed 6 people in a group at a time and we had way more than six at this meeting, so we couldn't hang out and talk. Besides, the order was given and it was non-negotiable. I was now the new chief of security. I will get into later what this position entails but in the meantime I needed to go see Rex and tell him what I thought about all this Jesus stuff.

As I got closer to Rex's cell I kept on playing through my mind what I would do and say once I go there. I was mad and I couldn't understand why something that is as popular as the Bible would be full of it. Once I got to his cell I threw the Bible at him and I said, "I am done with this crap." I went on to tell him that Matthew, Mark and Luke had different accounts of how many angels were at the tomb when Jesus rose from the grave. Matthew says there was one angel and he came from Heaven. Mark says there was one angel sitting in the tomb and Luke says there were two angels. "Can you

146

explain this to me?" Rex was kind of used to me having a real bad attitude about certain things and when I would get mad I would always take it out on him. He was the one who was involved with almost every aspect of my life and the more God was changing me the more I wanted to hold on to the past.

Rex got off his bunk and grabbed two pieces of paper and two pencils. He walked out into the hall way and said, "Do you see those two guys down there talking by the bathroom?" I said I did. "I want you to look at those guys for one minute. I want you to observe them and I will do the same thing. When we are done we will write what we observed them doing." I went to go say something and he said shut up and watch. Once the minute was up I wrote down what I saw them doing and Rex did the same. When we were done we compared our notes. I couldn't believe what I read. We both observed these two guys doing the same thing and our stories were completely different. Rex said, "Now since that is the case do you think it's possible that everyone who was at the tomb saw different things? Their best friend Jesus was just murdered and now he's not in the place that they buried him and on top of that there are angels sitting and standing around talking to them. They witnessed things in 3 days that the world has never seen. Some might have showed up at different times," he said. "But no one really knows."

I looked at him and said that's good enough for me. I walked into his cell grabbed my Bible that I had thrown and said, "See you at dinner." Every time I had a hard question Rex had an answer. It might not have been what I was looking for but he was always honest and if he didn't know the answer then he said he didn't know. I respected him for that and I continued on down the path of trying to learn as much as I could from him. But it wasn't easy for Rex to teach me. And one day he had enough of me and was heading towards my cell to tell me he couldn't be my friend and teacher any longer.

Being a gang member inside prison is very difficult but being a ranking gang member takes on a whole other meaning. I can seriously sum up in one word what my job as chief of security meant: babysitter. I was a glorified high ranking babysitter. When you see shows on TV about life in prison or how gang members operate you are only seeing the highlights. If the TV show didn't show the stabbings or murders no one would watch it. That's the society we live in today. But what the shows don't show is the day to day operations of a gang and it's not as violent as you might think. Yes we had days that were absolutely crazy where people got hurt. There were days that you would sit back in your cell at night and think, "My God what am I doing here?" or think, "Am I going to die tomorrow?" There were so many nights that I prayed Psalm 91 over my life.   Particularly Psalm 91:5-8. "You shall not be afraid of the terror by night, nor of the arrow that flies by day, nor of the pestilence that walks at noonday. A thousand may fall at your side, and ten thousand at your right hand but it shall not come near you. Only with your eyes shall you look and see the reward of the wicked." I recited that because I was living in a violent world and at any given moment I could be killed by other gangs, the gang I was in or by some nut job that just didn't like me. There were plenty of days that I looked into the eyes of someone and it was blank.   Some of these men were straight up ruthless killers. Some were child molesters who had raped two and three year old girls and others were down and out drug addicts who got themselves sent to prison for stealing. But if you back the gentlest person into a corner they will come out fighting, and you never knew who it was that wanted to fight.

Once I became COS I started to change a few things around. I was responsible for what my brothers were doing at all times and I was also responsible for handing out discipline to the ones who didn't want to follow the rules. For instance we had a no hard drug policy. You were only allowed to smoke pot. If you were caught doing anything harder than pot than you received a violation. The violation consisted of one or two minute beatings. I said before that we never punched in the face, so the one minute beating might be body shots. Other less severe violations might be standing on the yard for a few hours at a time watching over everyone. In the winter time that sucked because you would have to stand in the cold for hours without ever moving.

Because I was responsible for this and I wasn't a violent person by nature, I made sure that guys got every chance not to get the violation of beatings. I hated having to do that. One time I had to violate a friend of mine and the orders came from the top. He kind of screwed something up but it really wasn't a big deal, at least to me anyway. But they wanted to use him as an example and I had to do it. I went to this guy's cell and told him that whatever I did he could never repeat it. He looked puzzled. I took one last look around and ran up in his cell and punched him one time in the chest as hard as I could and dropped him to the ground. When he got back up he figured he had two more minutes of this and I said, "Nope, we are done." That guy thanked me for three days after that.

I really could never bring myself around to beating someone up I liked. Don't get me wrong though, there were times that I did become very violent and I let them know how mad I was by knocking their front teeth out, but back to the babysitting part. Every single day I would have to meet with people and solve their problems. Some instances were so minor and stupid I would just shake my head. One guy was playing basketball and the other one pushed him so now he wanted permission to kill the guy. Other times the situation was more serious but still never warranted someone getting stabbed or killed over. Pretty soon I had the reputation on the prison yard that I was fair and I wanted peace. There was a time for about 3 months that things were seriously getting out of hand between the different gangs and it needed to stop. The correction officers would only let so much go by them before they had to intervene. It was becoming hard to live because every day the officers would shake down our cells just to make us mad. They would take all our stuff and throw it into the hall ways and then mix it up with the guy locking next to you. I had enough of all this and I decided we needed to have a meeting with all the different gang leaders.

On a Saturday morning all the leaders from the different gangs meet out on the yard for what was known as a collation meeting, the first of many. At this meeting all our differences were discussed and we all had an understanding that if there was a problem we would try to talk it out before action was taken. It was unbelievable how much the petty violence went down. The officers were very appreciative and they lay off of us. And the leaders of the gangs started to respect one another.

Now don't get me wrong, this didn't always work but at least efforts were being made. This is why I said earlier that God was the one who promoted me to this position. Because of the change that God was doing in me, I was able to take that change and show people what God could do with someone as worthless as me. It even got to the point where if we were supposed to have a meeting Sunday night, the other guys would say we couldn't have it then. Scott goes to church.

Just before Rex was about to get off his bed and come down and tell me he was through with me, he said, he had a vision of him and I standing side by side. In the vision he saw himself taking his hand off my shoulder representing him walking away from me. And then he said he saw Jesus taking his hand and placing it back on my shoulder and telling him not to walk away. "I am changing his heart", Jesus said. Rex told me this when we were going to dinner one night and he had tears in his eyes. He said, "Scott I don't know what God has for you, but it is big because I seriously couldn't stand looking at you for one more second." That night I apologized to Rex and asked him to forgive me. From that moment on, I respected Rex like I never had before, and our relationship went from student and teacher to best friends.

During my free time from the gang, Rex and I would study and I mean study. Through all the different books we had I was getting an education in the history and times of Jesus. We would study the maps of Jesus Journey and figure out how long it took him to get from point A to point B and things like that. The only thing that I can compare our studying to is when I was a kid and I would go into my closet and study the baseball cards for hours upon hours. There were times that if we weren't done studying and we had to lock down for the night we would finish our study in the bathrooms.

In prison you were able to buy 13" black and white TV's, and the prison provided basic cable. Every morning I would watch a different TV evangelist and learn what they were

151

teaching and try to apply it to my life. A lot of the TV preachers were full of crap and only wanted money, but not all of them, and the ones who were sincere were the ones I held onto like my life depended on it, which it did by the way. One of the cool things about Rex was he would never talk bad about any of those people on TV. He said, "God would handle them," but he always made sure he knew who I was watching and he would show me in the Bible how they were wrong. One day I came to him and said, "I was watching a certain guy on TV." I didn't know it at the time but Rex knew the guy was full of it. After about 2 months of watching him I told Rex, "That guy is crazy. All he does is lie." Rex said he knew that about him, but he wanted me to come to my own conclusion. That's how Rex was. He was the real deal, and I wanted to be like him; but he wanted me to be like me, and over time he taught me how to be just me.

I can't stress how powerful the word of God truly is. When Rex and I would study the Bible or different books about Jesus and the history, I wasn't doing it to change my life. I never sat down and said, "Okay God, change me." I studied because I wanted to know more about God and who He was. The more I studied though, the more I changed. The more I read the words in the Bible the more it became real to me. I would actually sit back at night and think about how I would have acted as one of Jesus' disciples. Probably the same way I treated Rex, I thought. The change didn't come over night but day by day I would think about something and be like, "Hey I don't do that anymore." Sometimes a change would occur and I wouldn't notice it until sometime later. I had an officer tell me once that whatever I was doing I should keep it up because he liked my attitude. That's a huge compliment coming from an officer, and I told Rex what he had said. Rex told me that it was time to learn how to put my faith into action.

I really didn't understand what he meant by that but I said, "Okay I'm ready." The first thing was I needed to be baptized. The prison chapel had a Jacuzzi that they would put on the prison yard and guys would get baptized in that. I was baptized as a child because my parents were Catholics – or one was anyhow; so seeing people get completely submerged in a Jacuzzi was new to me. It actually kind of freaked me out but I knew that God wanted me to do it. One month later it was time to get baptized. I got into that tub and they dunked me for what seemed like an eternity. I guess I had a lot of sins that needed to be washed away. Once I came up out of that water I felt like a new man. I knew that getting baptized wouldn't get me out of prison. I knew that studying the Bible wouldn't either, but after that day I now had what Rex has had along and that is the peace of being right where you are. I didn't care that I could possibly have to be in for another 5 or 6 years. I just wanted to be with God. God used this baptism in another way also. There were so many gang members from different gangs watching this and they just thought I was crazy, but they respected it. One major gang leader from a Mexican gang told me later that he was proud of me for doing that and wanting something better for my life. He too wished for a better life. Although I never saw him change for the rest of my time in prison, we did have a few deep discussions about life.

Nineteen
THIRD CHANCES

Every 12 months I had to go in front of the parole board to see what they were going to do with me. Up to this point I had already done 3 years, and I knew that when I went in front of them this time around nothing would change. I figured they would just keep on giving me one year at a time until they couldn't keep me any longer, which was about another 5 ½ years. I didn't care though. I knew God had a plan for my life and if it meant being in prison for 5 ½ more years than so be it. That statement though is easier said than done. Every day I wanted out of that place, but I learned that I had consequences to pay for my actions. Yes I was forgiven for everything I had ever done up to this point, but that did not mean that I was forgiven as far as society went; and society kept me in prison. Society was about to have its day with me once again and its representative was the parole board.

I hated this day more than any day throughout the year. I knew what they were going to say, and I figured why waste all of our times. Just mail your decision to me without seeing me and we can all get on with our lives. Rex taught me though that no matter what, I needed to go in there with a good attitude and even though they could care less, I needed to talk about the change that Jesus was doing in me. When Rex told me that, I just laughed because I could only imagine the stories the board gets every single day 100 times a day about how someone has changed their life. No one in their right mind goes in to one of those meetings and says, "You know what? I'm still an idiot. I think that if you let me out I will rob the first bank I see." I knew though what Rex meant. Even if they didn't let me out this time around there is always a chance in another 12 months, so I needed to act like a child of God and not some immature goofball like I had in the past. I needed to go in there and be respectful, again, easier said than done.

The morning that I had to go in to see the board was absolutely horrible. The last thing I needed to hear was how I was still a menace to society and that there isn't enough rehabilitation in this whole world to help me. I didn't really pray about that day because I knew what they were going to tell me, but in the back of my mind I wished it would be different. One of the morning shift officers who I was cool with came up to my cell and said they were ready for me over at control center. "But before you go there," he said, "I want you to know that I believe in you. You have been in this block for 3 years now and I still remember the day you came in. You are not that same person, and no matter what I am very proud of you." I said, "Thank you." It meant a lot to me hearing this man say that. I had a very good relationship with 95% of the officers in the block I was in, probably because I was in there for 3 years straight like the officer said. The officers are doing time with you also but just on the installment plan. For 8 hours a day, five or six days a week they are there, and you get to know them.

There was one officer in particular who used to call me by my first name and if no one was around I also called him by his first name. We were friends but in a different way. Neither

155

one of us ever crossed that line between convict and officer, unless you want to call him bringing me a mountain dew every once in a while an example. But I ran into that officer many years later on the outside, and it was nice just to be able to chat with him. He said he knew I would make it and never return to prison. I wished I could have taken all those people who had nothing but good things to say about me into the parole hearing, but I couldn't; so I said one quick prayer and went in.

The parole process works in one of two ways. Either they are sending you home or they are not. When you meet with the board they usually don't give you a decision on the spot. They tell you that they will mail their decision to you, and you will have it within 30 days. Those 30 days sucked for every single person who was going through this. You could always guess on what you thought they would do or say, but no one ever really knew. I saw guys go home that had no business ever being let out of prison; and then the guys I thought should be let out would do year after year without going home. I was one of about 15 guys going in front of the board that day and I had to sit out in the control center visiting room until they called me in. About an hour into this I heard them say, "Mason, come on in." As I sat down, I noticed that only one of the members was there from the last time I came before the board, and the other two I had never even heard of. I hoped that this could work to my advantage. The one new member spoke up and said, "I have read your file and you have 36 felony convictions. Can you tell me why you have so many?" The other member who was new said, "Mr. Mason there is no way on God's earth that I will vote for you to go home. Besides your record indicates you are a known high ranking gang member and you are a menace to society." I thought, "Are you sure you weren't here last time. I heard those exact words before."

I spoke up and told her exactly how I felt about her comments and I also told her, "If God wants me out of here then there is nothing you can do to stop that." The third member who had been there the last time when they saw me said, "Mr. Mason, please step out of the room while we convene about this." This was kind of unusual, and it had never happened to me before, so I didn't know what to think. About 20 minutes later I went back in and sat down. The one that had nothing but bad things to say about me spoke up first. "Mr. Mason, I was impressed with how you handled yourself when I told you what I thought of you. You seem very genuine, and I am voting that we send you home." The other two spoke up and said basically the same thing. "Good luck Mr. Mason, and don't ever let us see you back in here again." As I walked out the door back to my cell I really didn't know what to think. I was still confused by what had just happened, and it didn't seem real. Did they say they were sending me home? Nah, I was just reading in to it. But they did say that I'd better never come back. Once I got back to my cell it was count time and everyone was locked up. I just sat back and thought about what just took place word for word, and I finally realized they were sending me home.

Once count time was over I ran to Rex's cell and told him the good news. I should have thought about this before I did it. Even though Rex was at peace about being in prison for life, it didn't mean he never dreamed about the day he might go home. Everyone in prison dreams about that day. The judge could have given you 240 years in prison and you will still hold on to the hope that someday you just might get to make it home. The other thing I didn't think about was Rex was about to lose his best friend. He was really happy for me, but I also saw the sadness in his eyes.

Once a person receives a favorable decision from the parole board to go home, it takes up to six months for everything to go through. This is by far the hardest six months for any person to ever go through in the prison system, and even harder if you are a ranking gang member. One of the conditions the parole gives you is that you are not to get into any trouble before you go home. If you so much as get caught taking a piece of fruit out of the chow hall, they will take away your parole and give you another 12 months. The other problem is a lot of guys in prison, especially the one I was in, are doing many years or life sentences. Once they find out that someone has a parole they are jealous, and some try very hard to get you to blow that parole. Don't ask me why people act like this, they just do. But one of the cool things that happened to me was the gang I was in wanted to see me go home; and they were going to do whatever it took for that to happen.

Twenty
NO CHOICE

Rex was putting his teaching into over drive. Not only did we study together every free second we had, we started a Bible study in the recreation room of our block at 10 o'clock at night. We probably had 10 guys every night come down and read God's word and just talk about how the Bible fit into our everyday lives. I grew a lot as a Christian at this point because I was now helping other guys see what I found out awhile back. Jesus is the real deal and if you allow him to he will change you from the inside out and give you a purpose for living, even if it is in a 6'x9' prison cell. One night as we were about to get started a friend of mine came and sat down beside me. He said, "Scott is it alright if I study with you guys." The reason why he was asking was because he was a ranking member of the Nation of Islam. He and I had become friends a few years back, and we never cared that I was white and he was black. We had a lot in common and we built our friendship off of that. I told him of course he could join us and he started to attend every night like the other guys. For the next few months I saw God making some drastic changes in his life. He hated white people for the most part, and now he was seeing first hand that white people weren't that bad. I asked him one time, "How is it you hate white people but you like me?" He said, "How is it you hate black people but you like me?" He had a good point, but now we knew that we really didn't hate people because of the color of their skin. It was just something that we both were taught at a very young age. If I could say I had a second friend whom I really cared for, it was this guy, and when it was time for me to go home we both were pretty sad because our friendship was about all we had in life.

Many years later my wife and I were watching the evening news and the top story was about my friend. He had always talked about how his wife divorced him while he was in prison and that really hurt him. She told him that he would never see his kids again and so on. That's real tough on an inmate because there is nothing you can do because you are locked up. I watched so many guys over the years come into prison and get a visit every weekend from their wife and kids for about a year and then it went down to every other weekend to once a month, and then the divorce papers came through the mail. It was too hard for someone on the outside to deal with, and even though they had every intention of being faithful they always found someone else to comfort them. The news caption for my friend went something like this. Parolee only out of prison for 3 days kills ex-wife and her two children. I came to find out once he was paroled and left prison he went looking for his ex-wife to kill her. He ended up stabbing her and her two children to death and let his daughter live. When I found all this out I kept on thinking back to the days he was with us at Bible study. I knew this guy had changed. I would have bet my life on it. But I guess anger over broken love got the better of him and he didn't know how to handle it any other way.

Back when I first started doing time a lot of the prisons I was in had one man cells; but as prisons started to become overcrowded they put two men in a cell. One of the guys I had in my cell was a convicted drug dealer. This guy was busted for major weight, meaning he was arrested for a lot of cocaine, so much that he received a life sentence for it. Tony was about 65 years old when I first met him and for the most part he was very quiet. He was not a part of any gang, but he was widely respected because of his drug ties in the world. After a few months of living with each other we figured out who does what and when. Tony loved to work out in the morning and he would run 5 to 6 miles a day. When he came back in from his work out, I would leave the cell and give him about an hour to himself. In that hour he would go down and take a shower and then come back up and drink his morning coffee. We did this seven days a week, and it wasn't real hard to figure out what our schedule was.

One morning Tony went down to take a shower as he usually did and I went to the yard. Our cells were operated by a key and each person had a key to their cell. When you took a shower you would generally hide your key in your towel and go into the shower area. The area where you would get dressed and place your towel was out of view of the actual showers so somebody could steal your towel and walk away without you ever knowing it until you got out of the shower, and this is exactly what happened. Two guys who had just come to the prison a week before saw our routine and decided to steal Tony's key and rob our cell. Once I came back in from the yard I saw Tony standing by our cell and asked him what was the matter. He said he must have lost his key and he was waiting for me to open the door.

Once we got in there we knew that he didn't lose his key because all of our store goods were gone. Between the two of us, we probably had close to $200 dollars in items from the store. At this point it was almost count time and we couldn't get the word out that we had been robbed until after lunch. Besides, when something like this happened to people like him and me, a whole lot of people get involved. One thing inmates hate more than anything is a thief inside prison. Kind of ironic isn't it? Also because of my gang status and having so many other friends in different gangs and Tony having all of the Hispanic gangs on his side, these guys who did this really didn't stand a chance.

Once word got out that we were robbed it seemed like everyone knew about it including the officers. The officers really didn't care because it meant more paper work for them, so they let us handle it. They also knew that we would find out who did this before they ever could, and they were right. The next afternoon we found out who the two guys were. Their cell was directly across from ours, and that's how they knew our routine. What they didn't know was who they were robbing. They thought I was just some stupid white guy too scared to do anything and they saw Tony as an old man. Once these two guys found out who they robbed they knew that things were about to get real bad for them and quick. So they went to one of the leaders of a black gang. The leader of the black gang and I were pretty cool with each other and we always had an open line of communication. He called me out to the yard that day and told me that these two guys asked his gang for protection, and he told them that they would not protect them and they were on their own. He said, "Do what you got to do to them."

I went back in my cell that afternoon and asked God why he was allowing this to happen. He knew that I had to take care of this problem and I was about to turn a few months left in prison into 20 years. I had no choice but to go after these guys. I had to make an example out of them and if I didn't I would have been in some serious trouble with every other gang member on the prison yard. Also this type of mentality was drilled into me. It didn't matter if I was going home in 24 hours. I still would have to take care of this and do it the only way I knew how.

That night at dinner we had a plan in place, and I and another gang member were going to get these guys on the prison yard that night. We had the plan all the way down to what to do if we got caught. The whole way through dinner though I kept on asking God to protect me. I said, "Please Lord, I don't want to hurt anyone else again, but I have no choice. You have to intervene." I recited Psalm 23 and Psalm 91 over and over again in my head. After dinner we all convened on the yard and set everything up. I and the other guy who was with me went looking for these guys, and we had only one thing on our minds. We looked all over the place and I kept on thinking, please Lord, help me. Just then one of the soldiers for one of the Mexican gangs said that they had those two guys over by the baseball diamond and the leader of the Mexican gang wanted to see me. Once we got over there, the leader pulled me aside and said, 'Look we know you are going home and we want to see you go home. This crap here isn't worth doing 20 years for. The 2 guys that did this have all your stuff and they are going to give it back once we are done here. Let us deal with this, and you go about your business." I thanked him, and I said, "Thank you, God," all the way back to my cell. Not only did God intervene but he used the guy who wished he too could have a better life the day I was baptized in the Jacuzzi.

The 10:00 PM Bible study that Rex and I had didn't stop just because I was going home the next morning. We gathered in the recreation room as we have had in the past, and we continued on with our study in the book of Revelation. By this time though Rex had kind of distanced himself from me, and the reason for that was because he knew that this day was eventually coming and now here it was. He had started a few weeks back helping out some other guy who was interested in Jesus and the whole Christianity thing, and he knew that he couldn't possibly teach me any more than he already had in all these years of us being together. Once the Bible study was done we all said, "good night" and went to our cells. I knew I would see Rex in the morning so I didn't have to say goodbye right then. Once I made it back to my cell I knew I wouldn't be able to sleep, so I made myself a cup of coffee and sat back on my bed thinking about the last 3 or so years of my life. I had come such a long way from when I first came here to this prison. I thought back about how I was so mad at God for sending me not only here but to 4 Block, but now I was thanking Him for doing that. I couldn't imagine where I would be today if God would have answered my prayers about coming there.

That experience has taught me so much even to this day. I am very careful for what I ask God for. I pray that His will be done not mine, because mine will get me into trouble every single time. I also thought about how Rex showed me how important it was to tithe my money. He showed me the verses in Malachi 3:8-12. I will never forget tithing my money to a ministry I watched on TV every day for many years. I believed and still do believe in that ministry but when I would tithe it would be off of what I made working inside the prison which was $13.10 every two weeks. I used to send that ministry $2.62 every month. They probably thought I was crazy. I knew my money didn't make a difference in the world standards, but it brought me closer to God and it made a difference in me.

As I sipped my coffee I shifted my thoughts from the past to the future. I had no idea what was ahead for me. Who would hire an ex-con with 36 felony convictions? How was it going to be living with my mom and stepdad again? Would I be able to find a church that had 10 PM Bible studies? Would a church even accept me? I had all these things rolling around in my head and finally I just said, 'Lord you have been with me this far. Please don't leave me once I get out there." I finished my coffee and lay down to go to sleep. I had a long day tomorrow. I still had to go to the county jail for 6 months, and they would be there bright and early to pick me up.

At 8:00 AM I walked to the officers' station in my block one last time and said goodbye to the morning shift officers. They all had nice things to say, and every last one of them shook my hand. Rex was waiting for me by the door to say our goodbyes. We talked for a few minutes and hugged each other. We both knew we would never see each other again and that was very hard for both of us. But just before I left, Rex said something to me that I will never forget. And I use what he said in my ministry today. He said, "Scott, God has placed a very powerful calling on your life to help people who can't find help anywhere else. I believe that God will use your story to heal people all over the world. Be patient and allow him to work in you and through you." He said, "I love you," and that was the last time I saw him.

One of my favorite quotes is in a movie called Shawshank Redemption. "Remember Red, hope is a good thing, maybe the best of things, and no good thing ever dies." I hope that I get to see my friend Rex once again.

Twenty-One
ONE LAST STOP

Going to the county jail for six months wasn't a big deal to me. I knew that if I stayed out of trouble I would be out in five months. And if they were overcrowded then maybe much sooner, who knows. But leaving prison to go do time in a county jail is like leaving the Hilton hotel for some flea bag motel. There was nothing good about it. Once I got there though was settled in, they asked me if I wanted a job working in the booking area. I would be a trustee, and that meant that I would have my own cell on the trustee floor and we would be allowed privileges the rest of the jail could not have. Working in the booking area on the afternoon shift was by far the best job in the whole jail and because I was considered a serious ex-con the Sheriff officers who worked booking treated me with respect.

They knew that I would mind my own business, and if someone happened to fall on the ground because of an officers foot then so be it. Some of these guys would get arrested for being drunk and when they got to the jail they decided that they wanted to fight everyone around them. Sometimes they had to be dealt with differently than most people that came in there. My job was pretty simple and I loved it because it kept me on my toes. I had to make sure that all the new arrivals got their jail clothes which consisted of 2 pairs of pants, two shirts, a couple pairs of socks and one pair of flip flops. I also had to pass out the food trays to everyone that was down in booking, and I had to collect the trays when they were done. I hated this part of my job though because everyone wanted extra food and when I didn't give it to them they would call me, "bitch" or "Jr. Police officer." I used to calm myself down by thinking that if you would have called me a bitch 3 months ago, you probably would be eating through a straw for 6-8 weeks. But that's not the attitude God wanted me to have and He was teaching me a different way of life, even though it was inside a jail booking area.

Another reason the officers liked me so much was I used to scrub down and wax the booking room floor. I found out real quickly that no one ever stripped the old wax from the floors and they would just put new wax on top of all that. I took a course in prison and became certified in stripping and waxing of floors and how to mix the proper chemicals and so on. By the time I removed 20 years of wax and put the new coats on, it looked like a million bucks. There was one captain who was known as a complete jerk and honestly I am being nice. Everyone and I mean everyone, stayed away from this guy. One day he took me over to the other side of the jail to load up some riot gear into the back of the police vans and on the way back the back to booking he said, "Sprite or Coke?" I said, "Excuse me sir?" "Sprite or Coke?" he said again, and I said "Coke." He left for a minute or so and came back with a Coke from the vending machine and handed it to me. He told me not to tell anyone. The Coke was for taking such good care of the booking area floors. That Coke was the best drink I ever had in my life. I earned that drink but at the same time I gave all the glory to God, because if it wasn't for Him I wouldn't have gotten that Coke in the first place.

When you worked as a trustee inside the jail you never knew when you were going to go home. When you were within two weeks of being released you could request an early release, and that's exactly what I did. I had all the officers that I worked for sign off on this, so I figured I had a pretty good chance of getting out early. One morning about 10:00 AM they called me down to the booking area and they told me to grab all my stuff from my cell. I honestly thought I was getting fired when I went down there. I knew I wasn't going home because I just put the request in. But once I got down stairs to booking one of the officers had a smile on his face and said, "Go change out into your street clothes. They are letting you out in one hour." I was so excited. I don't think I ever felt so much joy in my life. It had been 3 ½ years since I had seen the outside world and I couldn't wait.

My sister who was going to pick me up once I got out had no idea they were letting me out a few weeks early, so I was kind of scared as to what was going to happen once I was free. I got changed out as quickly as I could and signed some paperwork. They told me about my parole officer and said, "Take care." The door they let me out by was the same door they brought me in through, which was pretty cool. I took about two steps and breathed in what inmates call free air. I had about $14 dollars in cash on me so I headed towards the gas station to first buy myself a Mountain Dew and second, call my sister from a pay phone. Once I opened my Mountain Dew and took a big drink, I looked up toward Heaven and said thank you. I think a lot of our problems in this country stem from the fact that we are so rich that we forget to thank God for the littlest things. To me that Mountain Dew was like a million dollars, and I wanted God to know I was thankful for it. I called my sister and she said she would be there within the hour. Heck I didn't care if it was within 10 hours. I was happy sitting on the curb drinking my soda. As I sat there I thought about the county jail I just came from. That time I spent in there was the best time I ever had doing time. Sounds crazy right? When I was growing up I always wanted to be a police officer and as I got older that dream never went away.

Now obviously the second I was convicted of my first felony my dream of becoming a cop went straight out the window, but God never forgot about it. When I started working in booking at the jail, I learned so much about how police officers operate. I was working with them eight hours a day and at times they treated me like I was one of them. I pretty much was an officer for all that time minus the gun. God knew that I could never become an officer but He gave me the next best thing, and I was so appreciative of that. That reality somehow gave me a little more insight to who God really is and how much He really does love us. As I sat on that curb I thought about Him running the world and then saying, "Time out, Scott needs me." I still think about that at times and I know that's how he works, well, minus the, "time out" part. It was time to start my new life; a life that I never knew existed until I met Jesus Christ. And I was ready to go.

Twenty-Two
ROAD BLOCKS

Walking into my mom's house was different to say the least. I thought for sure she would never allow me back into her home, let alone to live. She too saw something different in me, and decided to give me one last chance to get it right. Right from the beginning though, I had problems. The driver's license divisions in Michigan revoked my license for five years because of all the stolen cars. For some reason they decided to start that process when I still had a few years left in prison, so now I had to go three more years without driving. It's hard enough to get a job or go to school as an ex-con, but not being able to drive just made it that much harder. But I had no choice, and I had to deal with it. The following day I had to go see my new parole officer and I needed a ride. This was difficult over the next two years because the parole office was in one of the worst parts of Detroit, and no one wanted to take me.

The parole office was nothing like the others ones I was at in years past. The waiting room of this place was a dump, and it was just like being back in prison. It seemed like every time I went it was like a prison reunion for some of these guys. The worst part was every time you left this place, guys were selling drugs right outside the door. You could go in and see your parole officer, take your drug test and walk out and buy weed, crack, coke and meth. Something like 85% of parolees in Michigan are addicted to either drugs, alcohol or both; and the drug dealers knew that all too well. The only good part of all this was I had a very cool parole officer, and as long as you were doing what you were supposed to be doing she left you alone. As time went on she loved me because I was one less person she had to look after, and making her job easier made my life easier, and that's what it was all about.

I have to believe that almost every single person who comes out of prison wants to do the right thing. They don't want to end up back in prison, so they come out full speed ahead with goals and dreams. The problem is once they have to take a different road or they hit a brick wall so to speak, their goals and dreams go straight out the window. And when you're an addict the easiest thing to do, instead of facing those problems, is to get high. When someone decides to take this path their thinking is not about the long term. It's all about the short term. They say I will just do this line or smoke this rock just this one time and then I will figure out my problems. The second someone puts that thought process into their minds they are done, even if they haven't gotten high yet. They should just go straight back to prison and tell them let me back in, because if I'm not back today I will be back shortly. This is why something like 90% of parolees end up back in prison within two years of their release. I had to take one of those different roads right from the beginning, and within a few weeks I too would hit that brick wall.

I had to find a job near my mom's house since I couldn't drive, and day after day I would walk up and down the street filling out job applications. After about two weeks of no one calling me back, I heard about a job opportunity to become a trash collector. People laugh at that job, but they make very good money and being out in the cold and heat day after day is a very hard job. I was excited about this opportunity because I figured they wouldn't care about my past and I would finally have a job. That morning I got all dressed up and headed out the door. The walk was about four miles away but I didn't care just as long as I had a job on that walk home. When I found the place I walked up to three guys that were waiting for work to start and I asked them when the manager would be in. I didn't need to hear their answer because all three of those guys were smoking a joint and they didn't seem to care who knew. I had a decision to make and it had to be quick. Do I stay here and try to get this job knowing full well I will soon probably be smoking pot with them, or do I leave and hope to find something else. I turned around and walked out. This was the brick wall I had hit. This job was my only hope since no one else would hire me. I remember walking home and I seriously had tears flowing from my face. I asked God where He was in all this. "What's going on up there? Are you too busy to pay attention to me?" Just then an 18 wheel truck came flying by me and as he went buy his truck hit a mud puddle and sprayed mud and water all over me. I was beyond mad. I was beyond any emotion because there were too many going on at one time. I thought all the way back home that I need to go back to prison because at least in there I was somebody. I can get a job with no problem, and I will not have trucks splashing me with mud. I was seriously through, but God wasn't and he was about to come through in a major way.

When my stepdad came home that night he could see in my face that I was giving up. He said, "Hey I know you probably don't want to be an electrician, but I can get you a job wiring new houses. And it's in the city I work in so I can drive you to work every day." I told him, "Of course I would want that job." Not only did I need a job, but being an electrician is a career and one that pays very well. One of my problems with getting a job by my mom's house was it wouldn't be a career type job, so I would be in trouble in no time at all. I needed to start whatever career I was going to do now, not later.

The next day I started my new job as an apprentice electrician. I never really thought about doing this as a career. When we were kids, we worked with my stepdad since he owned his own electrical company, but that was about it. After a few months of working at this company I really started to get the hang of it, and I loved my job. It was also a very serious job, because people's lives were at stake if we screwed up. The last thing we ever wanted to do was burn someone's house down, so everyone in the crew took their job seriously. I also became very good friends with a few of the guys I worked with. No one ever judged me for my past, and usually they wanted to hear my prison stories. The group of guys I worked with like to work hard and play even harder, and quickly I was caught up into their world. This was one of those times in life were I needed to be taught how to act like an adult and not an ex-con who liked to party. Looking back on some of these occasions, I see God was allowing me to continue on the way I was going but with a very short leash. I wasn't doing drugs, but I did start drinking and hanging out at strip clubs with one of the guys I worked with. He and I would hit the clubs every Friday and Saturday night. That lasted about six months and then God said enough is enough, and He reeled me back in. During this time I learned a lot about myself and my core values as a Christian. I wasn't having sex with women because I am a strong believer in abstinence. And

I really didn't care to drink, so I needed to figure out why I was hanging out with this guy. I think a lot of it had to do with the fact that I was lonely and the guy/guys I was hanging out with didn't judge me when everyone else did.

At this time I was going to church on Sundays, and I tried to become a part of the small groups the church had and meet people; but I had nothing in common with any of them and it never worked out. I always had the attitude it was me versus them. Also a problem I had was that my age did not match my maturity level. I spent 10 years locked up in prison away from the free world and everything it has to offer. My learning experiences were all from prison and that set me back many years; but I don't think that people who knew me could ever see that. They would just say Scott's very immature, and they wanted nothing to do with me. I have learned throughout this experience that a person can have every good intention of wanting to hang around the right crowd, but if that crowd doesn't accept them then they will go off and find someone who will; and usually that's not a good thing.

One of my favorite quotes from a friend of mine is this: "Who you hang out with will determine your future, good or bad." That quote is so true. I was also learning that just when I thought that all was lost, God would show up. Every single time that things would get hard it seemed like God wanted to see what I would do; and if I made the right choice He let me be. And if I didn't, He allowed me to travel down that wrong path just a little and then would come to get me. But before He would come to get me, He needed to introduce to me to my future wife. You would think that God would use a church gathering or maybe a library for us to meet and we would live happily ever after; but this is me we are talking about. And there is nothing American pie and white picket fences about me.

I started to really distance myself from the friend I was hanging out with. His drinking became too much for me to handle, and I realized this one night while we were headed home from a bar. He ran a red light at a major intersection at about 65 mph. I had never seen my life flash before my eyes as they say, but that night I did. I had had enough, but one Thursday night he kept on calling me and asking me if I wanted to go out to eat at this bar that was by my house. He promised he wouldn't drink; he just wanted to eat. Reluctantly I gave in and headed for the bar.

When we were done eating I happened to walk past this girl who was sitting with some friends, and I kept on looking at the guy she was sitting next to. He was overweight and in my mind he had no business being with such a hot girl. I saw her get up to use the bathroom and I followed her. Once she came out I asked her who the guy was, and she told me that he was a friend from work, but they weren't together. I went with her to where they were sitting and pretty much kicked him out of the way. Remember that at this point in time I hadn't quite arrived yet when it came to being courteous. I asked her what they were doing that night, and she said that they were all going back to this guy's apartment to hang out and drink. She asked me and my friend if we wanted to come over there. And I said, "Yes." I kind of felt bad for this guy, because instead of asking him if it was okay I just kind of showed up at his place. I still had a lot of issues to deal with when it came to certain situations like this one. Most people would have asked the guy if it was okay to show up at his place and if he said no, then they would be okay with that. If I had asked and he had said no, I would have showed up anyway, and then whipped his butt in his own home for being that way. That was the prison mentality in me, and God needed to knock it down a notch in a hurry before I got myself into trouble.

That night went fine, though, and there were no problems. She and I went for a walk, and for some reason I told her almost everything about me. I told her about how God got a hold of me in a prison chapel and how I really wanted to spend my life serving Him. She began to cry when I was done, and I remember thinking, "This can't be good." She went on to tell me about her life. She had a real bad experience in the church and had walked away from the whole God thing for a while; and her life was kind of spinning out of control. The cool thing about all this was God was using me to reel her back in. He had a plan for her, and it was not running around from relationship to relationship and to party after party. His plan was to draw her and me together through both of our experiences. And for what? – only He knew the answer to that.

About a month after I met Carrie, I asked her to marry me. I knew without a shadow of a doubt that God had put us together, and I wasn't going to waste any time asking her to be my wife. She and I lived about 40 minutes away from each other and since I wasn't allowed to drive yet, she had to do all the driving, which was hard on her. By this time I had moved out of my mom's house to a one bedroom upper flat, and I asked Carrie to move in with me. I knew that God had put us together and we were getting married in June so I saw nothing wrong with this. She moved in and we started playing house.

Around this time I started to get a little more involved with the church and I really wanted to speak to the teens in the youth group. I asked many times if I could, and they just kept on putting me off. One day I found out why that was. Some of the youth leaders felt that Carrie and I shouldn't be living together before we were married and they thought that sent a bad message to the teens. I was so mad, and I told these people to mind their own business. All I wanted to do was share my life experiences with these kids, and the church said no. "I'll do my own thing, then," I thought, "and I will talk to these teens one on one."

That was another problem I had back then, and sometimes still do to this day. I had a problem with authority. I had someone telling me for 10 years when to eat, when to shower, when to get up and so on, and I sure wasn't going to allow some church going people to tell me what I could do and couldn't do. So what they did was go to God with this problem in prayer, and in return God went to me.

I generally never have a problem when God speaks to me. I have a loving fear of Him. When He speaks I know I had better listen. One Sunday morning when I woke up God told me very clearly, "Either get married now or Carrie has to move out." I knew I had to do something, so I told Carrie what God had said and we had to make a decision. The cool thing about the people who were complaining about this was they were not really complaining. They actually loved us and wanted to see the best for us. They weren't trying to rain on my parade; they just knew what God wanted for us. Another thing they did and I learned a great lesson in this, was they gave us an option out. They told us Carrie didn't have to move back with her mom and dad who lived 45 minutes away. They invited her to stay with them until the wedding. Now that's putting your faith into action. They didn't tell the guy on the street who was hungry, "Get a job and we will be praying for you." They took action by feeding that guy and helping him in every way they could. The more I look back on that church and the people there, the more I miss it. I am hard pressed to find another group of people like them. The next day I went down and filed for our marriage license, and 3 days later we got married in the pastor's office. That was our first of three wedding ceremonies since we have been together. The second ceremony was three months later in June on the original wedding day that we had planned. And the third was our renewal of vows on our five year anniversary. Our good friend Pastor Tim did all three.

Twenty-Three
FAILURE IS NOT AN OPITION

Being married and having a promising career as an electrician was mind boggling for me. Not too many years prior to this I was playing gang member in a prison yard, and now God was taking me to places I never even dreamed of. It could have been really easy to stop here and enjoy life, but God wanted more for my wife and I. He had so much more to teach us and He was doing it Himself through different areas in our lives. Before I had Rex and a few other people who took me under their wing so to speak, and now it was God Himself. One of the things God wanted from me was to become a journeymen electrician. What this consisted of was 4 years of on the job training, which I had at this point, as well as being able to pass a test so hard that it's considered to be one of the hardest tests in the country. The test consisted of the three different fields in electrical-residential, commercial and industrial. Because I had done residential and very little commercial during my 4 years as an apprentice, I was at a huge disadvantage. You were allowed to use the code book during the test to find the answers but the code book is 1,400 pages, and you had only had 2 ½ hours to answer 82 questions. This was not an easy task by any stretch of the imagination.

Before taking this exam it was almost a must that you took classes that were offered to teach you what the exam would contain. In essence they would teach you what was going to be on the exam but you never knew what the questions would exactly be. The exam board went through great lengths to have three different tests on each site so that way no one could cheat or try to sell the exam questions to the next group. The class I chose was a weekend class, and it was literally 12 hours a day for two days. When I was done with that class, I had two notebooks filled with formulas and notes. I seriously didn't know if I was coming or going. I hated school and I even hated exams more, and throughout my whole school process from 3rd to 12th grade I failed probably 99% of every test I ever took. My thinking was there is no way that I can pass this. I only know about a ¼ of what this guy just taught. But I went home with all this information and busted my butt trying to study for it. My step father who owns his own electrical business is also an electrical inspector, so every time I had a question he would answer it for me. I studied every second I could, and when exam day came I made that 2 ½ hour drive to the site feeling pretty confident. That is until I sat down and looked at the exam. I tried my best to look stuff up but I kept on thinking about how much time I had left. When I was done with the exam I went back to the questions I didn't know the answers to and tried to answer them correctly. I started finding the answers and one by one I changed my answers. When I was done and it was time to turn the exam in I felt very confident that I passed this test just because I took the time to go through and change some answers.

They told us it would be about a month before we got the results in the mail. It reminded me of the parole process and how it took about a month to see if you were going home or not. This time though, I felt like I had a lot more riding on the decision. I needed to pass this exam because all I had done up to this point is fail at everything I had done. This was the true test in a sense. Becoming a licensed electrician wasn't the reason for studying so hard for this. It was so I could prove to myself and the world that I am somebody. I can and will succeed at what I put my mind to. On the 23rd day of the 30, my results came in the mail. I was nervous as I opened the letter.

My wife and I wanted to start a family and the one bedroom upper flat we were living in was way too small, so we decided to buy a house. The house we bought was a cute but very small 800 square foot house that had a huge beautiful back yard. We had a lot of plans for that backyard, but I never really got around to doing any one them. We were at a point in our lives that we wanted a lot of things but once we got settled with whatever we were doing we just left it at that. One thing I never "settled" on was helping people. I wanted more than anything to be able to have a backyard Bible study at the house we just bought. So I set off to find the people who were going to be a part of this. One thing I never understood once I came out of prison was why were things so different from the way we did them to the way the church does them. Here we had some of the craziest inmates in Michigan hanging out with us for no other reason but to get to know Jesus, but out here the people seemed to just use the church as a status symbol or a gathering to hang out with friends and family. I also never understood how the book of Acts could be so different than the way church is done in America. I started to get into a little bit of speaking, so I was able to see how different churches operated; and they all seemed to have the same theme. The theme I saw was they would help but only if it was during their schedule, didn't cost them any money, and if they didn't have to get their hands too dirty. I was hearing stories of churches that would actually tell people who had tattoos, piercings, and different hair colors not to come back the following Sunday.

That made me mad, and I started to hate what the church stands for in America. Now I know that all of the churches are not like that, but when you start seeing it for yourself time and time again it starts to wear on you. A few years before all this I asked God to give me the people no one else wanted. I wanted to help what society calls a lost cause, because I knew nobody is a lost cause. If that was the case then I would have been written off 20 years earlier. I also wanted to start this Bible study off somewhere where it had never taken place before; and I had my eyes on a very famous sports bar just outside of Detroit. I wanted us to meet there once a week for two reasons. First, I wanted to get everyone away from the idea that the only place to have a Bible study is in a church or some Christian's home. Secondly, I wanted others that were in the bar to see what we were doing, and hopefully if God was dealing with them maybe they would come over and see what was going on. The people we had that were attending our bar Bible study came from all walks of life. Some were drug addicts, some were recovering addicts, and others were everyday normal people on the outside, but on the inside they were dying.

The first time we had all of us together at this bar was so awesome. They had a bikini contest going on and 18 girls would walk around in their bikinis and try to get you to vote for them. It made a few of the people that were with us very uncomfortable because they thought this is not what Jesus would do. I said this is exactly what Jesus would do. He hung out with the sinners of the world. Once a few of the girls came over to get us to vote for them, their feelings on this changed. A few of the girls were excited we were doing a Bible study there and they too were Christians. And they talked to us about going to church and all that good stuff. I'm not too sure if we ever changed anyone's life outside of our group by going to the bar but who knows. I did know that it was time to start using the back yard we just bought, because we were growing in size and some of the people who started to come were alcoholics. And being in a bar around a bunch of alcohol was not the place to be if you had a problem with alcohol, even if it was in the name of Jesus.

I remember this day like it was five minutes ago. I pulled up into my driveway to get the mail. I had done this everyday for four days because I was waiting for my test results from the electrical exam. This day was different though. My exam results were there. I was so excited to open this letter that I was shaking. I opened the envelope and read the number 70. I wandered what that meant because right below it was the number 75. I had flunked the test by 5 points, which was equivalent to 2 ½ questions. I had so many feelings running through my head. I was so mad, and I felt like such a complete failure. "What am I supposed to do now?" I wondered. I knew I could take the test one more time, but if I failed it a second time I would have to wait two years from the last time I failed it before I could try again. I think I felt like that was an excuse. I thought, well if I don't take it again until I know I'm good and ready then I won't flunk it and have to wait two more years. I will just keep on studying and that will be that. I knew though that was a complete cop out. So I decided once and for all that not only would I study by butt off for this next exam, but I would also send in my paper work to take the next available test which was in about a month.

I knew I had a lot of work to get done, but I needed to find a quote I had once seen from Thomas Edison. He said, "I have not failed. I just found 10,000 ways that won't work," when asked about inventing the light bulb. I printed off a bunch of copies of that quote and put them in my text book, in my note book, in my wallet, and in my home. I must have seen that quote 1,000 times in a two week period. I also took off some time from work to study. I needed every waking hour I had to learn this stuff, and I'll be honest, it was extremely hard. When I was studying at home and found myself screwing around doing other things, I would leave and go to my mom's house and study in her back yard. I did this for two weeks and then got ready to take the exam.

The exam seemed to go no better than the first time I took it and failed, so this time around I just kind of shut my mouth when people would ask how I thought I did. I said I had no idea and tried to put it out of my mind. Once again I had to wait the 30 or so days to get the results, and around the 20th day I started looking out for it. One morning I was on a job with my stepdad, and I decided to head home real quick to check the mail. Once I looked into the box I saw the letter I was waiting for. I honestly didn't really expect it yet, but there it was. I had this letter in my hand and I wasn't nervous like the first time. I pretty much had it in my mind that I either passed it or I didn't. And if I didn't than I needed to figure something else out. The way I opened the letter I saw the score before I even got it out of the envelope. I knew I needed a minimum of 75 so when I saw a score of 81, I knew I had passed. I was officially a journeymen electrician. I had never accomplished anything on my own up to this point, and it felt so good to finally do something so positive with my life. I knew though that being an electrician wasn't Gods plan for my life. He had something else in mind for me and that something else would take me places I never thought in a million dreams I would end up. That included Hollywood Hills in Los Angeles, CA.

Twenty-Four
SOUTH CENTRAL TO HOLLYWOOD

I knew that my dream and God's desire for my life was helping people, but what I didn't realize was what needed to be done to make that a reality. I think when people see someone famous like an actor or musician they really don't know what it takes to get their name out there and make it big, and I didn't either. I decided to make a 20 minute CD about my life, and in order to do that I needed to ask a friend of mine who worked in Hollywood for many years to help me. One Friday night he turned my living room into a recording studio, and I asked my friend Tim to help us out. Tim would interview me and Steve would record. The CD turned out to be pretty good. I called it "Cage Made of Steel." Prior to this I had tried every method I could to get my story out there to the public. Tim actually wrote a letter for me and sent it to people he knew, and I also tried using cassette tapes instead of CD's. Even though I was home for many years, I still didn't really understand how multimedia worked. I didn't know anything about the internet, and in order for me to do the simplest tasks on a computer, I had to have other people do it for me. Once we got the CD done and I started to learn about the power of media, I knew I had to get a website up and running. What I didn't know was how much a professional website actually cost. My friend who did my CD recording also shot a two minute video with me about my life. This is what He did in

Hollywood and still does today. He shoots and edits videos. He did all this for free for me, but the song I wanted to use that went along with this video didn't come cheap. I knew that this was the song God wanted me to use and we needed permission from the artist to use it. We needed to contact a major rapper named DMX, and this wasn't going to be easy. It took awhile, but once my friend got in contact with DMX's agent, the negotiations began. He wanted something like $2,500 for like 30 seconds of his song. The problem was we were using more than 30 seconds and that obviously drove up the price. I couldn't afford $2,500+ so Steve explained to his agent that I just couldn't afford that. After a few emails and phone calls we got it down to $500, and she (the agent) explained thatI if we decided to sell it at any point then we needed to contact them and set up a new contract. I was cool with that because all I was doing with it was putting it on my website.

The next thing that needed to be done was the website itself. I contacted a guy who went to our church who built websites on the side. He was very good at what he did and I wasn't sure that we could afford him. Once we sat done and went through all the details he gave me a price of how much everything would cost to get it up and running and then how much it would cost to maintain it. I was overwhelmed. My wife and I surely didn't have anywhere close to that kind of money in the bank, so we decided to refinance our home. Please don't think that because we refinanced our home for God that it was a good idea. As a matter of fact, it wasn't, and it cost us in the end. But like a lot of times in my life I jumped ahead of God with good intentions when I shouldn't have, and he had to reel me back in. Once everything was said and done and the dust settled, I really thought I had everything I needed to do ministry effectively. I had a CD, website, videos, business cards and a will to get it done, but Scott was now running the show and not God, and when you reverse those two, well....

My wife and I were getting ready to go out on New Year's Eve when about 7:00 PM I received a phone call from my friend who did my CD asking for my help. There was a woman he knew out in Hollywood whose son was living in Michigan, and he was addicted to heroin. Her son was now in the hospital with an infection of some kind from using dirty needles and she asked him if he would go talk to him. He really didn't know what to say so he called me. I said, "Steve we are in the middle of a winter storm on New Year's Eve, and you want me to cancel my plans and drive 45 minutes away in this snow? Let's go. I will pick you up!" Helping someone is what I live for. I don't ever have to think about doing it. I figured if Jesus was willing to die on the cross for me then I surely can cancel some New Years Eve party for something as serious as this.

The meeting with this guy went just like I thought it would. He really didn't care what we had to say and he pretty much told us to leave. But I am a firm believer that one day if he ever gets his life back on track that he will remember the two guys who came to visit him on one of the biggest nights of the year, and he might just return the favor to someone else. About two weeks later I received a phone call from this guy's mom, and she wanted to thank me personally for going to see her son. She even wanted to send us some gas money which I thought was very nice. Over the next few weeks we talked quite a bit about her son and life in general and then one day she asked if I would speak to her small group that meets at her house every Monday. I said, "I would love to but I can't afford to come out to California." She said, "Don't worry about it; I will have my husband call you with the details." Right after I got off the phone with her I called my friend Steve and asked him if these people were on the up and up. He assured me that they were. He said, "They are some of the nicest people you will ever meet. Enjoy yourself out there; you will have a blast", he said. What Steve failed to mention was who these people were in the music industry and where they lived.

Once I landed in Los Angeles at LAX I grabbed my bags and looked for the lady with a sign. I had never met her before so she made up a sign that said "Scott Mason" on it. It was kind of cool because I felt like somebody. Once we got out of the airport we had about an hour drive in traffic up to Sunset Blvd. I had never been to Los Angeles but I knew all about it. I knew about Hollywood and all the cool places here and we were passing quite a few of them on the way to their house. Once we got onto Sunset I couldn't believe I was actually there. A lot of famous bands started their careers off there, and now I was right where they were. As we turned off Sunset we drove up this mountain, and she said, "This is called Hollywood Hills." Once we got to the top she parked her car. "This is it," she said. It was absolutely breath taking.

Up to this point I was so overwhelmed just by being in L.A. and now this. We went inside and I met her husband who is probably one of coolest guys I know. Keith said, "Go ahead and get cleaned up from your trip and when you're done I want to take you to Bel Air with me." He needed to go pick something up from an investment banker's home. That was probably the fastest shower I ever took. Fifteen minutes later we were out the door. As we drove down Sunset to Bel Air, we passed so many famous people's houses I think I had whiplash. Kcith said, "Look over there. That is Hugh Heffner's Playboy mansion, and over there is Hombley hills where a lot of famous people live." It seriously just went on and on, and then we turned down this street to where a bunch of armed men were standing. As we went through the gate he explained to me that those men were this man's security team. Once we pulled in and got past the trees I was in complete awe. The house was about 30,000 square feet and cost over $30 million dollars. In the driveway were a Bentley, Rolls Royce, and a Lamborghini; and on the other side of the driveway there were three more sports cars that probably cost over $200,000 a piece. I was introduced to the man whose home this was, and I really didn't know what to say. And then Keith spoke up and said I was from Detroit. They both laughed. They knew this was all new to me.

Once we were done we headed down Sunset to go eat. Keith chose a taco place to grab dinner but it wasn't an ordinary taco place. It was one that almost everyone in the area would go to at some point during the week. As we sat down outside I noticed a beautiful Mercedes Benz pull up and Christina Aguilera got out of it. I almost fell out of my chair. Here I am 20 feet away from someone I have been listening to on the radio for a few years. Keith started laughing. He told me that if I had a heart attack every time I saw someone famous then I was in trouble. He began to tell me who his neighbors were. Everyone from TV and movies to famous rappers and rock bands, and just then we were interrupted by a Lamborghini that pulled up on Sunset. The driver was Fergie from the Black Eyed Peas. I hadn't been here for 10 minutes, and I already had seen all these people. "Bring on the rest!" I told Keith.

Once we got back to the house, they showed me where I would be sleeping. My room and patio overlooked the Sunset strip and it was so awesome. Then they gave me the rest of the tour. In one of their rooms they had awards and plaques hanging everywhere, and the minute I walked into the room I knew what the two awards on the wall were. They were Grammy awards. The people I am staying with are Grammy award winning song writers! I didn't know what to think. Once the tour was done we sat back in their living room and talked about what I wanted to do that week and also talk about why I was really there. I was going to be speaking to a group of people that worked in the entertainment industry. I was told pretty much from the beginning of this conversation that whomever I would meet on Monday night and whatever was discussed could never go any farther than the living room. She didn't want me selling people's stories to the tabloids. I'm sitting there listening to all this and I am thinking, "Who am I meeting... Tom Cruise, Oprah?"

Well I can say that it wasn't them but it was people that are household names in some form or fashion. The group that I was speaking to was a group from the Mosaic church. Mosaic's pastor is Erwin McManus. Erwin and his wife Kim are friends with the people I was staying with. I had no idea who Erwin was at the time, but he is a very famous pastor and author and when I met him for the first time I would have never known it. They set it up that I would be speaking to a boy's home in South Central Los Angeles with a guy named Marvin. Marvin has quite a story as well. He is a famous music producer and at one time he was vice president of

Motown records. When I first went to his house I noticed all the awards he had also. He had a couple of diamond awards on his wall. Diamond meant over 10 million records sold; and they were from the record he produced for MC Hammer. Needless to say I had a very busy week ahead of me, but there was just one place I wanted to go and hang out at, and that was Malibu, Ca.

Malibu is famous for all its movie stars and rock stars that live there, but honestly I could care less. I was kind of getting sick of seeing all these stars because it would consume my whole day, and to be honest I wasn't a tourist any more. I was actually living next door to people like P-Diddy for a week or so. I needed to just chill and prepare for my speaking engagements, so I chose Malibu to do that. Every day I would drive down the Pacific Coast Highway and just marvel at God's creations: the mountains, the ocean, it was all so breath taking. I had picked out a real cool spot to do my work, and it was next to the Malibu pier which is famous in its own right. This is where they filmed a lot of the show Bay Watch. I had such a good time down there that I really didn't want to go back into the city. And every day I left to go back I would say to myself, "Someday I will live here." On my way home from one of those drives, I passed by where OJ Simpson lived and also where Nicole Brown and Ron Goldman were killed. And I thought to myself, "Even though people are rich and famous and have all this beautiful land around them, they still have everyday problems like people in Detroit. It really shows you that money does not buy happiness and fame is really just a pain in the butt."

Toward the end of my trip I was sitting in the pool enjoying the warm California sun and thinking about the last 10 days of my life. It was really too much to process, and I was warned about that when I first arrived. Keith told me that it would be overwhelming and I should just take it day by day. It was kind of funny but as I sat in that pool I thought to myself, "How can I possibly write about all this in my book?" That 10 day period could be a book by itself, and I really don't know how to talk about all that without it sounding like, "Look at me!" God really did use me out in Los Angeles, and that's why I was there. The rest was just a bonus from Him. I have gone out there on other occasions, and every single time it just amazes me how God uses someone like me to help people out there. There was one occasion though that God had to sit me down and basically say, "Look just because I send you out there doesn't make you any better than anyone else." And the way he showed me got my attention real quick. Today as I look back on all this I just smile and look up to Heaven and say, "Thank you."

Twenty-Five
GRACE FOR A REASON

I have lived in the Detroit area all my life. I don't think, besides my prison stays, I was ever more than 5 minutes away from where I grew up. It was time to get out of Michigan and start putting into action what God had been teaching us for so many years. One Sunday afternoon, my wife and I brought our daughter Erica down to my friend's church so he could dedicate her to the Lord. This pastor was the one who worked on my CD, and he lived about a block away from us in Detroit. Now he was the senior pastor at a church in central Ohio. After the service we all went out to eat before we headed back to Detroit. When we all sat down I heard God say to me that He wanted us to move down there. I thought about what I had just heard and kind of brushed it off. About two minutes later I heard the same thing. On the way home I told my wife, "I think God wants us to move to Ohio." She looked at me like I was crazy. If He did say that, then in order for that to happen, He will need to find a buyer for our house. At this time the housing market had already taken a hit and the $110,000 home we were owned was now only worth $35,000. When we got to Michigan we started praying about all this, and not too long after we started to put things in motion. We found a place to live in Ohio, but we still needed a buyer for our house. We had it worked out with the bank that we could short sale our house for $30,000, because they knew it wasn't worth the $110,000 anymore. So we dropped our price almost $80,000 and it didn't take long to sell.

There was one problem though. I had a job working with my dad in Michigan, and these projects needed to be finished; so once we moved to Ohio I was driving back and forth every weekend. I love to drive, so it wasn't all that bad, and I was so excited to see my wife and daughter. This went on for six months or so, and one day I received a call from an electrical company in Ohio that wanted to interview me. Someone I knew had a friend that worked at this company, and 6 months prior I had filled out an application not ever thinking anything of it until they called. It was time to be full time in Ohio...full time husband, dad, and employee. I was kind of upset with God though because I wanted so bad to go into full time ministry, and now I still had to be an electrician. As time went on, though, I understood why God had me at this company, and every single day was a new learning lesson for me that I would surely take into my ministry. I always had a problem with authority and working with others, and I prayed a lot that God would help me in that area. He did just that by promoting me to a manager of the residential electrical division at the company I worked for. God knew I wouldn't do all this on my own so he put me in a position that I had no choice but to follow authority and work with others. It was a tough go the whole time I was there, but I was truly changing, and that was good enough for me.

Over the years I have asked God, "Is it time yet for full time ministry?" and God would say very loudly, "No!" I wanted to serve God every day of my life, and being an electrician was not helping the matters. We worked very hard and long hours as electricians, and when I would finally get

196

home the only thing I wanted to do was eat, spend time with my family, and go to bed. Also, being an electrician meant that we would work on holidays because the plants that we serviced were off of work and that was the only time we could get in. It was more than just a full time job; it became 24 hours a day, seven days a week, with no time for God. I couldn't live like this any longer, and I wondered how much more God had to teach me before he would allow me to work full time serving his people.

The day finally came and it had God written all over it. I jumped out of the boat and started to walk on the water, but this time I didn't sink as I had in the past. I was finally in tune with God's timing. Now that didn't mean that I wouldn't screw up, but in the past I was always way ahead of Him when he would tell me to do something. A great example would be someone telling you that they are going to build you a foundation to build a house on but instead of waiting for that foundation you start to build on the dirt. Eventually and probably pretty quickly that house will fall down and you will have to start over. I built that same house on the dirt for years and every time it would fall I wouldn't wait for the foundation. I would just build it again right where I did before. This time though I waited for that foundation and I started to build upon that.

One day while I was coming home from Michigan, I happened to be listening to a radio station I never even heard of, and this guy had a radio show called 'Do Not Keep Silent.' I listened to the whole hour and called my wife and said, "Please write down this guy's ministry website." When I got home that night I checked it out from top to bottom. It was a little too conservative for me, so I basically just forgot about it. Then about a month later a woman comes up to me at the church I attend. She said, "Hey I want to introduce you to a guy named Jason. I think you two would work well together." She went on to say, "I think he has a radio show called 'Do Not Keep Silent.'" I just smiled. When we got home I found Jason on Facebook, and he and I became friends.

Jason's ministry, "World View Warriors" has a lot of different avenues. He books speakers and bands for conferences and one day events, and he also has that radio program. When we first met he really wanted to use me as a speaker, but he had a hard time believing that everything I told him was true. Most people don't have a story like mine, and it is kind of crazy. Jason went to my website and found my reference page. I don't have the phone numbers to some of the people on there because of who they are; but upon request I will give them out. Jason took it one step further and never asked me for the numbers. He found out on his own what the numbers were and called these people. What he found out was that the story I was giving him indeed matched up with people who have known me for years, and he was excited. We started to work together and hang out quite a bit. He interviewed me for his podcast, and I was on his radio show quite a bit. One of the episodes we talked about was the EF-4 Tornado that hit Lake View and Millbury, Ohio in June of 2010. Right after that happened I went up there to help people out. What I witnessed firsthand was complete and utter devastation beyond anything I could imagine. Seven people died the night of that tornado including a family named Walters. The Walters never saw the tornado coming, and it obliterated their house along with several others that were in the path of the ¼ mile wide tornado. The Walters' seven year old daughter, Madison, somehow survived and she had to bury her dad, mom and little brother. A few days later I stood where their home once was. I have been a part of a lot of things over the years, but this disaster changed my life in ways I cannot even describe. In all, over 50 homes were leveled to the foundation, another 50 were destroyed. The city hall/police department and high school were destroyed.

One of the first homes that the tornado hit and destroyed is now rebuilt, and I have become friends with that family. Every once in awhile I go over there and talk with them and see how things are going. It goes to show you that in the matter of seconds your life can be turned upside down and we must live life like it's going to end at any second.

Jason became my sole booking agent and over a period of time he tried to put together a few different tours for me to go on; but because I wasn't well known, very few people booked me. I also believe that God was behind this because we would get people to say, "Yes bring Scott in," but then they would back out at the last second. I had a lot to learn about all this, and God was using Jason to teach me.

Finally one day Jason called me up and said I have you booked for a 6 state 4,000 mile tour starting off in Callaway, MD. He was also going with me on this trip because he felt that God was telling him to teach me about the road; and I will tell you that I am glad he did. If I wasn't speaking, we were driving and that was the whole trip. He said when we were done with the trip that it represented the most miles he had ever driven in such a short amount of time. Even though the trip was long and very difficult at times, I still had a blast. It was the first time that I was able to help teens and adults across the country in person, and I think that is so important.

One of my favorite places that we went to was Concordia University in Seward, Nebraska. It was the second time I would be speaking to a University in a matter of a month. When we arrived there, they had my name posted on every billboard and bank around. They really wanted to promote me because they have a very serious drug problem in and around the city, and they figured people would listen to what I had to say.

I had to speak twice that night, and the first group I spoke to was a teen home for kids that were in trouble and real close to going to jail or prison. I love talking to kids like that because we have so much in common and they know we do, so they listen. The second group of people I talked to was at the university itself. They had me in a hall with about 250 seats. Before we got started they had to get another 150 or so seats because the place was filling up quickly. That night was cool on so many different levels. Here I was, kicked out of 3 high schools, one college and obtained my GED in one of the toughest prisons in the country, and now I am speaking at a very well known university with no degree of any kind on my wall. As I walked out of that university I thought back to the night in the prison chapel, the night that God touched me and I would forever be changed. I said, "Thank you," to Him for that night, as I wiped a tear from my eye.

Epilogue
HAROLD

In the months leading up to this book I have spoken to thousands of people across the country. I have done numerous radio interviews, and I have written several articles about my life through blogs and websites. All those things I just mentioned are great but to be honest, the 2:00 AM phone calls I get because someone is in trouble are what keep me going. I love to get involved with someone's life on a personal level. When I am done speaking I hand out my personal cell phone number and tell people to call anytime, day or night. I sometimes think people call just to see if it is actually me on the other end, and they are shocked when they find out it is. To me this is what ministry is all about – being there in the tough times of someone's life. Not just feeding them if they are hungry, but actually getting to know them while they eat. Taking time to ask them how they are and truly meaning it. I have learned over the years that a lot of times people don't want you to fix their problem; they just want someone who will listen. And listening doesn't cost you a dime but it's worth a million dollars to them.

I asked God a long time ago to let me help the people who have no hope in life whatsoever: people who are so down and out that they are one step away from suicide either by choice or because of the drugs they are doing. Drug and alcohol addictions in this country are at an all time high, and it's not just the people who are living in the hood. These people are our doctors, lawyers, school teachers, and stay-at-home moms. They fly under the radar because no one would ever suspect them, and if we aren't taking the time out to ask how they are doing ,then how will we ever know until it's too late that they have a problem?

I have a story with which I would like to finish this book. It is a story of how two men from very different walks of life can have one thing in common. I met Harold in prison way before I saw him standing on the front steps of the church I attended. Harold was a gang member from a gang that was always at odds with us, but he and I would see each other at the Sunday church service we had in prison. We hit it off pretty quickly, and we always had something to talk about other than prison life. Harold was about 50 years old when I first met him, and his face looked like he was 65. But he did keep in shape by working out. Harold was in and out of prison his whole adult life due to the heroin addiction he had.

One day while we were talking he told me that he loved Jesus more than anything in his life but that he just couldn't seem to kick this heroin habit, and he was scared that he was going to end up in hell. I told him, "Harold, God knows your heart, and that is that." "Yeah," he said, "But the church people tell me that I am going to hell if I keep this up." I said, "Harold, are you praying every day for God to deliver you of this habit?" He said, "With all my heart, soul, and mind." And I said, "Do you believe that God is hearing you?" He said, "Yes." "Then leave it at that," I told him. When I saw Harold standing on those steps, I have to be honest, I hadn't thought about him for many years. And I felt bad because I should have been praying for him.

As I approached him I saw in his eyes he was doing what he has been doing for 30 plus years, and that was getting high on heroin. He looked like crap and smelled pretty bad too. I said, "Harold come on downstairs and let's get you cleaned up and fed. I know you have to be hungry." When he was eating we talked about the old days in prison and how it has changed since I was there. We talked about his mother and how he promised her he would quit heroin before she died. That really bothered him because he loved his mom so much and he broke his promise to her. And we talked about the upcoming NFL football season. When he was done he asked me for some money so he could grab a bus back towards the shelter he was staying at. I usually never give money to addicts, but to me Harold wasn't an addict. He was a follower of Jesus Christ who for some reason couldn't kick this habit. As I walked him out he said, "You know Scott, the whole time we were downstairs eating you never once judged me for where I am at in life, and you never once told me that I needed to change, and I love you for that, brother. I don't think I ever told a white guy that I loved him before so you are probably the first." I said, "Harold it is not my place to judge you. You know what you have to do to get your life back on track. I think you have been in this cycle for so many years that you don't know anything else. My job as a follower in Christ is to make sure you are fed, warm, and loved on in a way you never have had before. The love of Christ is an awesome thing." He looked at me and tears were flowing down his face. And they weren't tears of sadness but tears of joy because he knew that Jesus loved him so much even if he was a heroin addict.

I helped out Harold quite a bit over a two year period, but he was busted for being in possession of heroin and was sent back to prison. Not too long after that Harold died of a heart attack while in prison. His body finally shut down from all the years of abuse. When I found this out I cried, not because he died, but because he never really got to live.

Contact Information:

If you would like to contact Scott:

E-mail:
totallycommitted4him@yahoo.com

Websites:
www.scottmason.org